EXPOSURE THERAPY FOR CHILDREN AND ADOLESCENTS

HELP YOUR CHILD CONTROL THEIR ANXIETY DISORDERS, PHOBIAS, AND OCD WITHIN 10 WEEKS

LULU JAMES

CONTENTS

INTRODUCTION

Anxiety does not empty tomorrow of its sorrows, but only empties today of its strength.

— CHARLES SPURGEON

Are you concerned about your child's behavior? Wondering if their tantrums are normal or if their defiance is a sign of something more serious? No one is born happy all the time. Feeling anxiety, fear, anger, sadness, and other emotions is perfectly normal. But when these feelings become too intense, they can interfere with a person's daily life. If you notice their fears and anxieties seem to increase, you might wonder if your child is developing an anxiety disorder.

Anxiety disorders are the most common mental health disorder in the United States, affecting about 7 million children between the ages of 3–17 (CDC, 2019). While it is normal for children to experience some anxiety, it becomes a problem when it interferes with their daily life. If your child is missing school, not taking part in activities they once enjoyed, or having difficulty making friends, it might be time to try exposure therapy.

Since the COVID-19 pandemic, children's depression and anxiety rates may have doubled. According to the Center for Infectious Disease Research and Policy, about 20.5% of children have anxiety compared to the 11.6% before the pandemic (McLernon, 2021). This increase is likely due to the amount of tension and uneasiness that comes with the uncertainty of the pandemic. When children grow up with excessive anxieties or fears, it can lead to developmental delays and social isolation. It can also affect their adult lives unless we provide them with skills and tools to help their management of anxiety.

Unmanaged anxiety can lead to depression, panic attacks, mental disorders, autoimmune disorders, gut problems like IBS and colitis, and even early-onset arthritis. It severely limits the quality-of-life learning opportunities and can become entrenched and totally define a person's life if not dealt with early.

Children's anxiety can manifest in different ways, depending on their age and development. For example, separation anxiety is a common worry amongst adolescents when they are away from their parents. School-age children might worry about doing well in school or making friends. Adolescents might worry about fitting in or being accepted by their peers.

There are several types of anxiety disorders, each with its own set of symptoms. However, a common practice to overcome anxiety and fears is to use exposure therapy techniques. This is a type of therapy that gradually exposes the child to the thing they are afraid of in a safe and controlled environment. For example, if your child is afraid of dogs, the therapist might start by having them look at pictures of dogs. Then they would progress to looking at real dogs from a distance. Eventually, the therapist would help your child work up to being close to a dog and maybe even petting one.

This type of therapy can be very effective in helping children overcome their fears and anxieties. However, the stigma and confusion around exposure therapy mean that many parents will not even consider it as an option when, in reality, if done correctly, it is anything but harsh or cruel. In fact, with the right approach, it can mean the difference between a fearful, unhappy child and an empowered, confident child who can tackle anything that comes their way.

Stigmas arise from the unknown and the unfamiliar. When we do not comprehend a challenge, it is easy to be afraid of it, which is why education and understanding are so important for managing anxiety and fears in children. The key is to understand how exposure therapy works and how to select the best therapist for your child, a therapist who needs to really know what they are doing.

We think by helping our children avoid their fears and protecting them from having to face these triggers, we are doing our best as parents, but research shows that avoidance creates a cycle of anxiety and fear reinforcement, making it all worse in the long run. So, instead of protecting your child from their fears, it is important to empower them by teaching them how to face their fears head-on.

We need to face our fears—which can sound both too simple and extremely hard—but to do so, we need help. A therapeutic process developed by people who understand how our brains work, which is proven to ease anxiety, is a good idea. This is not a do-it-yourself proposition. We need the help of an expert to rewire our brains and change our relationship to our fears.

However, by learning the skills and using the tools in this book, you will manage your own fears and how to help your child(ren) identify and manage their own fears as well. You will also be able to help your child(ren) receive the professional help they need with a lot more confidence and peace of mind, knowing that you are doing everything in your power to aid them.

One in eight children will have an anxiety disorder in their lives, so it is important to be informed and get the help you need if your child is struggling. With the right support, your child can learn how to manage their anxiety and live a happy, healthy life. This book has everything you and your child(ren) need to get started on the road to recovery. So, let's get started!

1

EXPOSURE THERAPY EXPOSED

D ue to a lack of information on it, there are not that many exposure-therapy clinicians and the belief that having patients directly face their fears will not ease their debilitating fears, panic, and worry. However, those who are trained in this form of therapy know that, when used correctly, exposure therapy can be very successful.

WHAT IS EXPOSURE THERAPY?

Simply put, it is a type of cognitive-behavioral therapy that prompts patients to confront their fears in a safe and controlled environment. The goal is to help them overcome their fear and anxiety so that they can live a normal, healthy life.

Exposure therapy has been proven to be an effective treatment for several anxiety disorders, including:

- Post-traumatic stress disorder (PTSD)
- Generalized anxiety disorder (GAD)
- Phobias
- Obsessive-compulsive disorder (OCD)

Research shows that exposure therapy is one of the most efficacious and powerful treatments available for these disorders. In fact, exposure therapy has been proven to be more constructive than medication for treating anxiety disorders.

One reason that exposure therapy is so effective is because it can help our children to confront their fears head-on. By doing this, they can learn that their fears are not as big or overwhelming as they thought. They also learn that they can handle their fear and anxiety, even when they are confronting it directly.

Another reason that exposure therapy is beneficial is because it helps patients to learn new coping skills. They learn how to deal with their fear and anxiety in a healthy way. This is important because it means they will use these skills in their everyday life, not just when they are in therapy.

Exposure therapy is a way to gain control of fear and pain by helping people rewire their brain responses to anxiety-provoking situations. This technique uses specific techniques that are not only based on fear-extinction learning but also new insights into the neurobiology of fear. These techniques are not harmful to children, nor do they require lengthy treatment times.

Exposure therapy focuses on either flooding or gradual desensitization. Flooding is defined as the patient being exposed to their fear all at once, with no warning. This can be very overwhelming for the patient and is not recommended for everyone.

Gradual desensitization is when the patient is exposed to their fear gradually. This means they start with something that is not too anxiety-provoking and then work their way up to the most anxiety-provoking situation. This is the more common way to do exposure therapy, as it is less overwhelming for the patient.

The techniques used in exposure therapy are:

Systematic desensitization: This is a process where the patient is gradually exposed to their fear in a safe and controlled environment. Similar to gradual desensitization, first, they start with a small fear and work their way up the fear ladder to their scariest anxieties.

In vivo exposure: This is where the patient is exposed to their fear in real life. This could mean going to the place they are afraid of or doing the activity they are afraid of.

Imaginal exposure: This is where the patient imagines the fear-inducing situation. This can be done by picturing it in their mind or watching a video of the situation.

Virtual reality exposure: This is a new form of exposure therapy that is becoming more and more popular. In this type of exposure therapy, the patient is exposed to their fear in a virtual-reality environment. This can be a very realistic way to confront their fear without actually having to put themselves in the situation.

Trained therapists understand the interplay between the comfort zone, the growth zone, and the panic zone. They would never intentionally put a client in the panic zone. The goal is always to help the client gradually move from their comfort zone into their growth zone, where they can learn new skills and strategies for dealing with their fear.

Exposure therapy is a promising treatment for anxiety disorders. It is a relatively new field, but the research that has been done so far is very promising.

HORROR STORIES AND STIGMAS

Sometimes horror stories get the best of us, which has led many people to believe that exposure therapy is a scary and dangerous treatment, but this is not the case. With the help of a trained therapist, exposure therapy can be a very shielded and productive way to deal with anxiety.

Some common myths are that exposure therapy is:

- Dangerous and cruel.
- Too much work.
- Only for people with severe anxiety.
- Only for people who have not responded to other treatments.
- Taking away our autonomy.

Exposure therapy is none of these things. It can help people regain control of their lives in a cautious and practical manner. Stigmas come from a lack of knowledge and understanding. While exposure therapy is still a new field, it is very promising. Educating ourselves about exposure therapy before making any decisions is crucial so that we can make the choice that is best for us.

WHEN IT DOESN'T WORK

Exposure therapy is not a cure-all and does not work for everyone. In some cases, exposure therapy can actually make anxiety worse. This is usually because the exposure is not done correctly or because the person is not ready for exposure therapy.

Common reasons exposure therapy might not work are:

- An improperly trained therapist

Make sure you see a therapist who is trained in exposure therapy and has experience treating anxiety disorders. Check their credentials, formal training, and experience before choosing a therapist. This is not something an amateur in the modality should undertake.

- The patient was exposed to something too scary, too soon

The exposure should be gradual and done in a safe and controlled environment. If the exposure is too intense, it can actually make anxiety worse and cause the client to become re-traumatized.

- Therapy was stopped too soon

Exposure therapy can be a lengthy and arduous process, but it is important to stick with it. If the exposure is stopped too soon, the anxiety will probably come back and never be completely defused.

Unfortunately, these are concerns that many parents face. However, these issues can mostly be avoided if we check and select our therapist carefully. If we know enough about the method, we can discuss the therapy plan fully before it is started.

Exposure therapy can be difficult, and working with a therapist you trust is important. Trust that the process will work if you give it time and be patient with yourself. Remember, your child is not alone in this. Many children and adolescents have anxiety, and many of them have found relief through exposure therapy.

HOW IT SHOULD WORK

Exposure therapy should be done gradually and in a safe environment. The therapist will work on creating a hierarchy of fears, starting with the least fearful situations and working up to the most fearful, then help the patient expose themselves to that specific hierarchy. However, before the therapist dives into exposure with their client, it is important to do some prep work.

Before the actual exposure therapy occurs, the patient must be taught relaxation and self-calming techniques. This is important because exposure therapy can be intense and difficult, and the patient will need to calm themselves down if they feel overwhelmed. They must be internalized sufficiently that they are second nature and can easily be accessed at any anxious moment.

The therapist should also teach the patient about anxiety and how it works. This is important because understanding can empower, and it can help the patient feel more in control of their anxiety.

SUCCESS STORIES

According to Effective Therapy Solutions, a 10-year-old girl, Sandy, became distraught with fear and anxiety. When her brother was diagnosed with asthma, she became fearful of getting sick. Sandy was weary of germs and was concerned she would get her brother sick one day, and it would be because of her.

As a result, she began washing her hands often until they were raw. This fear progressed into her education, believing that school was a breeding ground for germs and that if Sandy brought anything home from school, she would contaminate her family with germs.

Sandy also tried to implement these strategies on her family, requesting that they also wash their hands excessively or avoid germ breeding grounds. If they didn't abide by her rules, she would throw a tantrum, but they were soon growing frustrated and tired of her outbursts.

A psychologist met with Sandy and her family to help this young girl develop healthy coping mechanisms for when she feels anxious about germs. Through exposure therapy, the girl was gradually exposed to different environments and situations that would usually make her anxious about germs. Sandy learned she could be brave enough to face her fears and that her fears weren't as bad as she thought.

Eventually, Sandy's fears went away with each exercise. The therapist also taught the family how to enable a reward system with the exposure therapy so that the girl would be motivated to face her fears. The therapist helped this young girl see that her fear was manageable and that she could live a normal life without allowing her fear to control her.

Now, Sandy can go to school without fear and is no longer anxious about germs contaminating her or her family. Her parents are free from outbursts, and within four months, she was back to being a happy and healthy 10-year-old girl who enjoyed going to school and spending time with her brother.

According to Advanced Behavioral Health, an 8-year-old girl, Sarah, started having intrusive thoughts about her sister drowning in the family swimming pool or taking the steering wheel to run someone over. She knew something was wrong. It all started after a new kid at school had bullied Sarah. Suddenly, she was avoiding anything that might trigger these upsetting thoughts—television, swimming pools, even driving in the car.

Thankfully, Sarah's parents were understanding and helped her get the help she needed. After being assessed by a therapist, it was determined that Sarah had OCD. This type of anxiety disorder occurs when people have undesired thoughts, images, or impulses that make them feel uncomfortable or scared and recurs often.

Sarah became compulsive. She would compulsively jump over cracks and doorways or repeat actions in sets of four. She developed simple motor tics like smelling her fingers, scrunching her lips, and symmetrical tapping to relieve the physical tension that these obsessions created.

Sarah's OCD worsened over time until it significantly impacted her daily life. However, she reported significant improvement in her obsessive thoughts after a short-term course of exposure therapy and response prevention. The young girl was no longer avoiding her stressors and found the images and thoughts to be boring. Her tic-like behavior stopped as her anxiety decreased and habit reversal techniques were used. Within three and a half months, the girl and her mother reported that OCD was no longer a concern for her.

If your child is displaying any similar behaviors, seek professional help as soon as possible. OCD and other anxiety disorders can be debilitating disorders, but with the right treatment, children can learn to manage their obsessions and compulsions and live happy, healthy lives. It's difficult to watch our children suffer, but with the right help, they can overcome their fears and anxieties. The first step is determining what is really going on in a scared kid's mind.

2

WHAT ARE CHILDREN SO AFRAID OF?

A child's fear is a world whose dark corners are quite unknown to grownup people; it has its sky and its abysses, a sky without stars, abysses into which no light can ever penetrate.

— JULIEN GREEN

Anxiety is a normal part of childhood development. Children with anxiety disorders often suffer in silence because they're afraid to tell anyone about their fears, or they don't understand what they're experiencing.

Children can be afraid of many things: the dark, animals, clowns, heights, blood, needles, thunderstorms, germs, and even death. Most of these fears are developmentally appropriate and will eventually go away on their own.

However, if a child's fear is excessive, lasts for over six months, and is causing notable distress or impeding their daily life, it may be an indication of an anxiety disorder.

Many anxiety disorders can affect children. The most common are:

Generalized Anxiety Disorder (GAD): Children with GAD worry excessively about things like school, their health, or the safety of their family. They may have trouble sleeping and may feel nauseous or dizzy from the anxiety.

Separation Anxiety Disorder: This is when a child experiences extreme anxiety away from their parents or guardians. They may refuse to go to school or sleep away from home.

Social Anxiety Disorder: Children with social anxiety disorder are anxious about being around people. They may worry about embarrassing themselves or being judged by others. This can make it hard for them to make friends or participate in school activities.

Phobias: A phobia is an intense fear of a specific thing or situation, such as heights, dogs, or flying. Children with phobias may avoid their fears at all costs, which can interfere with their daily life.

WHY DO CHILDREN SEEM TO HAVE SO MANY FEARS?

There are many theories why children seem to have so many fears. One theory is that they haven't developed the cognitive ability to understand that their fear is irrational and that they're safe.

Another theory is that children are more in tune with their emotions and are more likely to experience anxiety because of their heightened sensitivities.

It's also possible that children have more fears because they're exposed to more things that can be scary. With the rise of the internet and social media, children now have access to things that they wouldn't have been exposed to in the past, such as violence, natural disasters, and death.

In a general sense, children are young and still trying to decipher their world. There's a lot that's unknown to us, so imagine how confusing and scary it must be for a child. To a young child, there's a lot they can perceive as a potential threat, and if something makes little sense in terms of what they know already, it can trigger acute anxiety.

Another aspect to consider is that anyone who experiences trauma when first being introduced to something can hardwire the brain to create a fear trigger. That is why some children might be afraid of things like lawnmowers, clowns and other dressed-up characters, fluffy toys, noisy toys, and even cartoons.

THE AGES AND STAGES OF CHILDHOOD FEAR

Unfortunately, we as humans can experience fears at any age; even babies experience anxiety or fear. Most children start to experience fear around the age of two. This is when they understand things can be scary and that they're not always in control. Fears usually peak around the age of six or seven and then slowly decline as children get older.

There are four main stages of childhood fear.

The first stage is called the "stranger danger" stage. Children are afraid of people they don't know and cling to their parents or guardians during this stage. They may also be afraid of animals, loud noises, and unfamiliar places. This can be especially true for babies around eight months. As they recognize faces more, they may also become attached to a specific person, such as their mother or father.

The second stage is called the "fear of separation" stage. In this stage, children are afraid of being away from their parents or guardians. They may have trouble sleeping in their own bed, going to school, or being in public places without a parent or guardian.

The third stage is called the "fear of beasts" stage. This stage is when children are afraid of animals, such as dogs, snakes, and spiders. They may also be afraid of the dark, ghosts, and monsters. This can also be referred to as the "pretend stage" since children at this age may use their imagination to create fears.

The fourth stage is called the "fear of natural disasters" stage. Children are afraid of things like thunderstorms, tornadoes, and earthquakes during this stage. They may also be afraid of heights, bodies of water, and getting lost. This is typically the last stage of childhood fears as children understand more about the world around them.

Additionally, social fears have become more prevalent in recent years, with children now being afraid of things like public speaking, social media, and bullies. This usually occurs in the teen years as they're trying to navigate their way through adolescence.

While fears are a normal part of childhood development, some children may experience more intense fears than others. If a child's fear is obstructing their daily life or causing them distress, it may be time to seek professional help. A therapist can help a child understand their fears and develop coping mechanisms to deal with them.

WHAT DOES FEAR FEEL LIKE FOR A CHILD?

For a child, fear can be a very overwhelming and confusing emotion. It's hard to understand why something is scary or why they're feeling afraid. Fear can cause a child to feel isolated, alone, and helpless. They may also feel like they're not in control of their own body or emotions.

No matter the trigger, fear feels real, threatening, and an enormously overwhelming emotion for children. Fear can manifest itself in many ways, both physically and emotionally. A child may experience a racing heart, shaking, sweating profusely, and shortness of breath. They may also feel dizzy, lightheaded, or nauseous.

Emotionally, a child may feel anxious, worried, or scared. They may also experience a sense of dread or foreboding. In some cases, children may even feel like they're in danger or going to die.

Keep in mind that fear is a natural emotion. It's a way for our bodies to protect us from harm. However, if a child's fear is intense and overwhelming, we might feel the need to push our children to face their fears. This can actually do more harm than good.

If the child feels unsafe, forcing them to face their fears can increase anxiety and worsen the situation. They can become re-traumatized, which will reinforce their fears. Children can lose their trust or faith in you if they are pushed too quickly or are forced to face their triggers against their will. This may lead to the child's anxiety being even greater than the child's current feelings. They might feel they are entirely alone and cannot trust you to help them.

Outdated parenting techniques, harsh discipline, punitive behaviors, and misguided notions can promote fear in children, but creating and promoting fear is probably the worst thing a parent can do. Positive parenting is a better option.

Positive parenting is focused on the positive aspects of a child's behavior. It rewards good behavior and ignores destructive behavior. This type of parenting can help reduce fear in children by teaching them that their parents are ready to support and encourage them.

Some ways to promote positive parenting include:

- Encouraging your child when they display positive behaviors.

- Praising your child for their successes.
- Showing empathy and understanding toward your child.
- Setting clear expectations and consequences for negative behaviors.
- Providing a safe and secure environment for your child.
- Being patient with your child.

Be supportive and understanding. Let them know that you're there for them and offer reassurance. Help them understand what they're feeling and why. Allow them to take small steps at their own pace in order to slowly confront their fears.

COMMON CHILDHOOD FEARS

Young Children

Most young children have fears of the dark, ghosts, and strangers. They might also be anxious about dogs or other large animals, bugs, heights, or blood. Other common examples include flying, going to the doctor (especially if shots are involved), loud or unfamiliar sounds and imaginary fears like the monster in the closet or the "thing" under the bed. These fears are common and usually subside by age six or seven.

School-Age Children

School-age children often fear doing something wrong or being embarrassed in front of others. They might also have fears of school, tests, or bullies. Many children also have separation anxiety at this age and may fear being away from their parents. These fears usually subside by age 10 or 11.

Adolescents

As children progress into their teen years, their fears become more "grownup" and indirect. Adolescents often have fears of not being accepted or not fitting in. They also might have fears of failure or not being good enough. The fear of their parents divorcing or of natural disasters can also be common. Other common adolescent fears include drugs, alcohol, sex, peer pressure, and getting in trouble. These fears often persist into adulthood.

While some fears are common and developmentally appropriate, other fears might be a sign of an anxiety disorder.

WHAT IS THE DIFFERENCE BETWEEN A FEAR AND A PHOBIA?

Fear is a normal, developmentally appropriate emotion that all children and adults experience at some point. Fears usually subside within a few minutes or hours once the threat is safely contained and do not interfere with daily functioning. On the other hand, a phobia is a tenacious and irrational fear that leads to avoidance or significant distress. Phobias can be divided into three categories:

- Animal phobias, such as the fear of dogs, snakes, or rodents.
- Environmental phobias, such as the fear of heights, storms, or water.
- Situational phobias, such as the fear of enclosed spaces or flying.

Phobias can debilitate and prevent people from leading normal, active lives.

WHAT IS THE DIFFERENCE BETWEEN ANXIETY AND AN ANXIETY DISORDER?

Anxiety is a normal emotion that we all experience at times. It is the body's natural response to stress and can be beneficial in certain situations. It can help us stay alert and focused, motivating us to take action. However, when anxiety becomes excessive, it can be disabling and interfere with our daily lives. This is when it becomes an anxiety disorder.

There are several anxiety disorders, including:

- Generalized anxiety disorder (GAD)
- Obsessive-compulsive disorder (OCD)
- Post-traumatic stress disorder (PTSD)
- Social anxiety disorder
- Panic disorder

Anxiety disorders are the most common type of mental illness and affect millions of people all around the globe. They are treatable but often go undetected and untreated. If you are concerned that you or your child might have an anxiety disorder, speak with your doctor or a mental health professional.

WHAT IS THE DIFFERENCE BETWEEN OCD AND ANXIETY?

While OCD and anxiety share some common features, they are two distinct conditions. OCD is characterized by obsessions (recurrent, intrusive thoughts) and compulsions (repetitive behaviors or mental acts that are performed to neutralize the obsessions) (Mayo Clinic, 2020). On the other hand, anxiety is a diffuse feeling of fear or apprehension that can be triggered by anything from everyday worries to more specific phobias. While anxiety can be debilitating, it rarely involves the same repetitive, intrusive thoughts and behaviors characteristic of OCD. However, the constant need to repeat behaviors or subside their thoughts can cause anxiety to develop in people with OCD.

What is OCD?

Obsessive-compulsive disorder is a mental disorder that is characterized by obsessions that are heightened and compulsions to help ease those obsessions (Mayo Clinic, 2020). OCD can be a very debilitating condition, interfering with work, school, and personal relationships.

It's also a common condition, affecting about 1 in 200 children (Obsessive-Compulsive Disorder in Children and Adolescents, 2018). OCD usually begins in adolescence or young adulthood but can also develop in childhood.

There are several types of OCD, including:

- Checking compulsions, such as checking the locks on doors or the stove.
- Cleaning compulsions, such as washing hands or cleaning the house, because they are weary of germs.
- Hoarding compulsions, such as collecting or hoarding objects.
- Symmetry compulsions, such as needing everything to be perfectly symmetrical.
- Counting compulsions, such as needing to count steps or objects.

In many cases, OCD is a brain disorder that runs in families, but it can also happen in children with no family history of OCD.

ANXIOUS CHILD CASE STUDY

According to ADAVIC, 10-year-old Hannah was described as "anxious from birth." Hannah had been a shy, reserved young girl in preschool, but she integrated well in grade one. She made friends and succeeded academically. However, in the mornings, she started complaining of severe abdominal pain that was never present at night. Hannah missed about 20 days of school because of this pain. She would also avoid school excursions because she feared the bus would crash. She would constantly ask her parents for their reassurance and had difficulty sleeping alone.

From worrying about school tests to the possibility of her parents dying, Hannah struggled with anxiety. Although she had no history of childhood trauma, Hannah was clearly experiencing extreme anxiety, which was interfering with school and sleep.

It is perfectly normal for children to have fears. In fact, it is a sign that they are growing and developing. Most children's fears peak around the age of five or six but usually disappear by the time they reach adolescence. However, some children's fears persist into adolescence and adulthood. When a child's fears are excessive, constant, and interfere with their daily life, it may indicate an anxiety disorder.

Signs of anxiety can be wide and many but may include:

- Excessive worrying.
- Avoidance of certain situations or places.
- Difficulty sleeping.
- Irritability.

If you're concerned about your child and the possibility of them having anxiety, there are a few questions you can consider:

- Does your child avoid age-appropriate activities or situations? Or do they avoid them without you?
- Does your child have repetitive behaviors?

- Does the child worry or ask you for reassurance every day?
- Does your child complain about headaches, stomachaches, or experience hyperventilation?

If you answered yes to any of these questions, your child might experience anxiety. It's important to seek professional help, so they can learn to rewire their fears and live a normal life. They can implement well-renowned techniques that can assist your child in managing their fears and overcoming their anxieties. However, the next step is understanding why children have fear. So, what is the science behind our fears?

3

THE SCIENCE BEHIND FEAR

Ultimately, we know deeply that the other side of every fear is freedom.

— MARILYN FERGUSON

Fears are normal. Adults have them, children have them —everyone has a fear or two they're concerned about. However, children have to learn how to deal with their fears in order to grow up and become independent adults.

WHAT IS FEAR AND WHY DO WE HAVE IT

Fear is an emotion we feel when we think we are in danger. It's a natural response that helps us stay safe. When we believe we're in danger, our brains enter the "freeze" or "fight-or-flight" stage. This means our body gets ready to either fight the danger or run away from it. Fear causes our muscles to tense and our heart rate to go up, which is all part of the "fight-or-flight" response.

This response is the normal way our bodies protect us. Not all fears are bad. Fear can actually be helpful! It's what keeps us safe when we're in danger. The brain keeps us safe, and fear is one way it does that. The only people who don't experience fear or the flight-or-fight response are people with brain damage, psychopaths, or dead.

Fear can be traced back to our ancestors: the cave dwellers. When a cave dweller saw a lion, their body automatically went into panic mode. This helped them either fight the lion or run away from it. They didn't have time to contemplate their actions; they just reacted.

Additionally, cave dwellers needed to work in groups and have the best equipment in order to survive. This is because they needed to defend themselves and their food from other animals. They also needed to find a mate in order to reproduce and keep humanity alive.

These were fears that were ingrained into their brains and affect us today. The fight-or-flight response is still present in humans today. However, we now no longer have the same dangers or concerns our ancestors had, so those fears translate to other areas of our life. For instance, as cave dwellers, socializing played an important role in survival. Although that's not a primary concern currently, today's social anxiety can stem from the old fear of being rejected by our cave dweller ancestors.

These fears are helpful to an extent, but as we get older, our perceived fears can drive a lot of dysfunctional behavior if we don't realize they're no longer useful. Nonetheless, we now have the ability and knowledge to think and reason, which means we can control our fear.

The "fight-or-flight" response is still hardwired into our brains today. However, sometimes fear can get out of control. When fear is excessive and constant, it can be a sign of an anxiety disorder.

The "fight-or-flight" response differs from an anxiety disorder. This response is normal and meant to protect us, so it only happens when we're in danger. An anxiety disorder is when someone feels anxious all the time, even when there's no danger. This can interfere with their daily life.

TWO INNATE FEARS

According to CNN, a study in 1960 revealed that children and animals have two innate fears: falling and loud sounds.

Falling: Babies as young as six months old will scream when they're falling, even if they're not hurt. Researchers believe this is because our ancestors who didn't have this fear didn't survive long enough and couldn't pass their genes to children.

Loud Noises: All animals are born with a fear of loud noises. This is because loud noises can signal danger. For example, a loud noise might mean an animal is coming to attack.

These two fears are innate, which means we're born with them. However, we also develop other fears as we grow older.

DEVELOPMENTAL FEARS

Developmental fears are fears we develop as we grow and learn about the world around us. Developmental fears are normal and expected. Most children go through a phase of being afraid of the dark or afraid of monsters under the bed. These are all developmentally appropriate fears.

Children typically develop new fears as they learn more about the world around them. For example, a child who has never been to the beach before might be afraid of the ocean. Once they learn more about the ocean and see that it's not dangerous, their fear will go away.

Other developmental fears can include extinction, mutilation, loss of autonomy, separation, death, or ego/loss of identity.

Extinction: This is the fear of annihilation or non-existence. It's the fear that we will cease to exist, either physically or mentally.

Mutilation: This is the fear of physical injury or damage. It can also be the fear of losing a body part.

Loss of autonomy: This is the fear of losing control. It's the fear that we can no longer make our own decisions or take care of ourselves.

Separation: This is the fear of being separated from someone or something we're attached to. It can also be the fear of being alone.

Ego: This is the fear of losing our sense of self, such as fearing that we can no longer identify who we are.

Death: This is the fear of dying or ceasing to exist.

Most of these developmental fears are temporary and will go away as we learn more about the world and our environment. However, some of these fears can become long-standing if they're not addressed. Though, developmental fears are normal and expected. Children usually outgrow them as they understand more about the world.

LONG-STANDING FEARS

Some fears can become long-standing or chronic. This means they can be difficult to overcome and last a long time. Long-standing fears can interfere with our daily lives and prevent us from doing things we want or need to do.

Examples of long-standing fears can include social anxiety, specific phobias, agoraphobia, claustrophobia, and PTSD.

Social anxiety: This is the fear of social situations. It's the fear of being around other people and feeling anxious or embarrassed.

Specific phobias: A phobia is being irrationally afraid of a particular object or situation. Examples of common phobias can include heights, flying, needles, and spiders.

Agoraphobia: This is the fear of open spaces. It's the fear of being in a place where it would be difficult to get help if we needed it.

Claustrophobia: This is the fear of enclosed spaces. This fear arises when we are in a place where we might feel trapped, tight, or believe we're unable to escape.

PTSD: This is the fear of a traumatic event. It's the fear that we will re-experience a traumatic event from our past.

THE UNKNOWN AND LACK OF KNOWLEDGE

In some cases, our fears can be caused by the unknown or a lack of knowledge. This can happen when we face something unfamiliar. For example, if you've never been to the dentist before, you might be afraid of what will happen. Once you go to the dentist and see that it's not so bad, your fear will go away.

In other cases, our fears can be caused by a lack of knowledge. This can happen when we don't have all the information about something. For example, if you're afraid of flying, it might be because you know little about airplanes. Once you learn more about how airplanes work and what safety measures are in place, your fear will go away.

However, there are generally two types of fears: rational and irrational.

Rational Fears

Rational fears are based on real dangers. For example, it's rational to be afraid of flying if you're afraid of heights. It's also rational to be afraid of dogs if you're afraid of being bitten.

Irrational Fears

Irrational fears are not based on any real danger. For example, it's irrational to be afraid of flying if you're not afraid of heights. It's also irrational to be afraid of dogs if you're not afraid of being bitten. For instance, children might also fear dogs because of their fur or germs from their snouts—not just about being bitten.

Irrational fears are generally based on our thoughts and perceptions. For example, if we think all dogs are dangerous, then we might be afraid of dogs even if we've never been bitten.

Some irrational fears can be helpful. For example, if we're afraid of flying, it might motivate us to learn more about airplanes and how they work. However, other irrational fears can be harmful. For example, if we're afraid of dogs, it might prevent us from getting close to a dog and learning that they're not so bad after all.

CHILDHOOD FEARS VS. ADULT FEARS

Even though we share some fears with our ancestors, there are also many differences. For one, children tend to have more fears than adults do. This is because they're still learning about the world around them and what is safe. As they learn more, their fears will go away.

Some fears are specific to childhood. For example, many children are afraid of the dark or of ghosts. These fears are generally irrational and will subside the older the child gets.

Other fears are more pertinent to adults. For example, many adults are afraid of heights or public speaking. These fears are generally rational and based on the danger of the situation.

Some fears are common to both children and adults. For example, many people are afraid of snakes or spiders. These fears can be both rational and irrational. However, if these fears go on unprocessed or unmanaged, they can cause long-term problems.

UNPROCESSED AND UNMANAGED FEARS

Fears that continue on without being managed or processed properly create longer-term effects on children that can last into adulthood. Fear is a natural, adaptive emotion meant to protect us from harm, but it can lead to negative outcomes when it goes unaddressed.

Unprocessed fear in children can result in:

- Anxiety disorders
- Depression
- Post-traumatic stress disorder
- Substance abuse

THE IMPACT OF ANXIETY

Anxiety can be significant and long-lasting. However, you can manage your fears effectively by understanding how to deal with them.

If you have anxiety, you may:

- Avoid certain situations or places.
- Feel like you can't control your worry.
- Have trouble sleeping.
- Feel tired or fatigued.
- Experience headaches or stomach aches.
- Sweat or have a rapid heartbeat.

Prolonged anxiety can affect your physical health, memory, brain processing, and mental health.

Physical health: Prolonged anxiety can lead to high blood pressure and an increased heart rate. It can also debilitate your immune system, which makes you more prone to catching illnesses and more difficult to fight them off. It can lead to headaches, stomachaches, and other physical symptoms.

Memory: Anxiety can lead to forgetfulness and trouble concentrating. This can also make us more anxious if we can't remember what we need to do.

Brain processing: When we are anxious, our brain processes information differently. We might have trouble focusing on the task at hand and be more likely to make mistakes. This can make it tough to focus, think, and make decisions.

Mental health: Anxiety can lead to depression, which is a serious mental health condition. If left untreated, depression can have a damaging impact on your life. It can interfere with work, school, and personal relationships. It can even lead to thoughts of suicide.

Finding ways to cope with your anxiety is crucial so that it doesn't have a negative impact on your life.

THE EFFECT OF FEAR AND ANXIETY ON THE BODY

Anxiety is not all in our heads; it also affects our bodies. Fear and anxiety are natural reactions that have evolved to protect us from danger. The "fight-or-flight" response is a prime example of how anxiety or fear can affect us.

When we sense danger, our bodies prepare us to either fight or run away. This response is caused by the release of hormones like adrenaline and cortisol. These hormones help us be more alert and focused and give us the energy we need to face the danger or run away to safety.

The problem is that sometimes our bodies can get stuck in the "freeze" response, even when there is no danger. This can lead to physical symptoms like a racing heart, sweating, and difficulty breathing. It can also make thinking clearly or making appropriate decisions challenging.

Anxiety disorders can cause an accelerated heart rate, palpitations, or chest pains. These disorders can also prompt high blood pressure or heart disease. If you already have heart disease, anxiety disorders may raise the risk of coronary events.

Anxiety can also cause gastrointestinal problems like abdominal pain, diarrhea, and nausea. It can also lead to headaches, muscle tension, and insomnia.

We can create a habit of anxiety and fearfulness or create environments that promote anxiety, which we need to be mindful of. We can also hardwire our brains to be more reactive and easily triggered if we let stress and anxiety go unmanaged for any length of time.

The good news is that there are things we can do to manage our anxiety and reduce the symptoms. Exercise, relaxation techniques, and therapy are all effective treatments for anxiety. We talk about how to avoid this in later chapters because you cannot help your child calm down until you know how to relax yourself first.

4

CALM YOURSELF FIRST

The process of spotting fear and refusing to obey it is the source of all true empowerment.

— MARTHA BECK

I t is impossible to be calm and rational when your child is experiencing anxiety if you are also feeling anxious. In order to help your child, you must first manage your own anxiety. This may seem like a laborious task, but it is possible with practice.

If you model self-calming techniques and behaviors, your child(ren) will also pick up on this and learn from you. Your thoughts create your feelings, and these create your reality.

What you focus on is what becomes real for you (and your child). When you learn how to master your thoughts, you can then teach that to others.

When you focus on your thoughts, you can change the way you feel. This is called cognitive restructuring—a powerful tool for managing anxiety.

Cognitive restructuring is identifying and challenging negative or distorted thoughts and replacing them with more realistic and positive ones. This can be done by first recognizing the thoughts causing you anxiety and then thinking about whether they are really true. Once you have identified the thoughts causing you anxiety, you can start challenging them.

For example, let's say you are worried about your child getting sick. You may think, "My child is always getting sick. I'm a terrible parent." These thoughts are not only negative, but they are also distorted. They are not based on reality and are not helping you feel better.

Instead of these negative thoughts, you could try thinking, "My child is healthy most of the time. I am doing my best as a parent." These thoughts are more realistic and positive and will help you feel better.

This may seem like a minor or pointless swap, but it can significantly affect how you feel. Once you challenge and change the beliefs triggering your fears, you will feel calmer and in control.

Of course, it is not always simple to alter the way you think. If you're a long-term worrywart, it may take some practice to learn how to cognitively restructure your thoughts. But it is worth the effort because it can change your life significantly.

THOUGHT DISTORTIONS

However, our thoughts are not always accurate or true. Sometimes, we have what are called cognitive or thought distortions. Cognitive distortions are ways that our thinking can get skewed or distorted. They can make us feel worse about ourselves and make it harder for us to solve problems.

There are a few different cognitive distortions. Some of the most popular ones are:

All-or-nothing thinking: This occurs when we see a situation as one extreme or the other—either good or bad. For example, if your child got a C on a test, they might think they are a failure. This type of thinking is not helpful because it doesn't allow for any shades of gray. They don't acknowledge how hard they worked or how they can improve—they focus on the extremes, which isn't an accurate portrayal of life.

Overgeneralization: This is another popular distortion when we make sweeping statements based on one insignificant event. For example, if your child got into an argument with their best friend, they might think that all of their friends hate them. This type of thinking is not based on any evidence but will contribute to more negative thoughts and feelings.

Mind reading: This distortion occurs when we think we know what someone else's beliefs or thought processes are—despite a lack of evidence. For example, if your friend ignores you, you might think they are talking about you behind your back. Or your child might be afraid to tell you something because they "know how you will act." This distortion usually lacks evidence to support the thought pattern and can cause more anxiety.

Fortune telling: This distortion happens when we think we know what is going to happen in the future, with no evidence. For example, if your child is about to take a test, they might think they are going to fail.

Magnifying: This thought process comes from when we make a minor problem seem bigger than it is. For example, if your child got a C on a test, you might think they will never amount to anything. This type of thinking is unhelpful because it is not based on any evidence and can also lead to self-esteem problems.

Minimizing: When we make a big problem seem smaller than it is, this is minimizing. For example, if your child stole a car, you might think it's not a "big deal." This thought process doesn't benefit us because it means we are not taking the problem seriously.

Labeling: This thought process is when we give ourselves or others a label based on one small thing. For example, if your child made a mistake, you might label them as a "failure." This distortion is also usually based on a lack of evidence and can lead to a lack of self-esteem.

Catastrophizing: It is when we think that an insignificant problem is going to have huge consequences. For example, if your child gets a C on a test, you might think they are going to flunk out of school. This type of thinking lacks evidence and can create more negative stigmas about the situation.

Personalization: This popular thought distortion happens when we think everything is our fault. For example, if your child gets in a fight with their friend, you might think that it is because you are a terrible parent.

As you can see, there are many cognitive distortions, and these are just a few of the most popular ones. It is important to be aware of these cognitive distortions because they can make the situation more difficult, affect our self-esteem, and affect our decision-making skills.

You and your child can experience any of these distortions. However, by learning to observe, analyze, and test our thoughts, we can change them. The first step is to notice these cognitive distortions so you can challenge them.

BECOMING AWARE

Now that you understand the different thought distortions you can have, you can notice them better. To notice and understand your thoughts, you can start by paying attention to your emotions.

Your emotions are like a "red flag" that goes up to let you know when you are having a distorted thought. For example, if you are feeling anxious or stressed, you are likely having a distorted thought.

Cognitive distortions are a part of life, and we all experience them from time to time. However, by noticing them, we can challenge them. This can help us feel confident and prompt us to solve problems more effectively.

Once you notice your thoughts, you can start to "label" them. This means you will identify the cognitive distortion and then label it as such. If your thought is an example of all-or-nothing thinking, you would say to yourself, "I am having the thought that I am a failure because I yelled at my child."

You can then start to "challenge" your thoughts. This means you will look at the evidence and see if your thought is really true. If you struggle with all-or-nothing thinking, you will challenge it by looking at all the times when you were a good parent, even when you made a mistake. All the times you didn't yell or get angry.

You can also use "reframing" to change your thoughts. This means you will look at the situation differently. You could reframe all-or-nothing thinking by saying, "I am not a failure. I am human. Everyone makes mistakes sometimes."

You can also use "affirmations" to change your thoughts. This means you will say positive things to yourself, about yourself. For example, you could say to yourself, "I am a good parent. I am doing my best. I am loveable."

You can also "change" your thoughts. This means you will find a more helpful thought to think instead of the cognitive distortion. You could reframe your thought to "I am doing my best. I am human. I will make mistakes sometimes. That's okay. I am still a good parent."

To challenge your thoughts, you can also use "logical reasoning." This means you look at the facts and determine if it really supports your thought. You will start by looking at the evidence and see if there is any evidence that supports your thought. You can also seek evidence that supports the opposite of your thinking.

You might find there is some evidence that supports your thought. For instance, yelling at your child might support your thought of being a "terrible parent." However, you might also find there is more evidence that does not support your thought, such as the patience you exhibit when they're making a mess.

Additionally, if you still struggle to challenge your thoughts, you can ask yourself questions like "Is it really true that I am a failure because I yelled at my child? What are some other ways to look at this situation?"

To help you keep track and identify your emotions, consider keeping an emotion chart or having regular discussions with your child during the day about how they are feeling. The more you talk about your emotions, the more your child will feel comfortable discussing their emotions with you and understanding them better.

It is important to remember that thoughts are not facts. Just because you have a thought doesn't mean it is true. You can choose what thoughts you want to believe. The power to control your thoughts is yours. You can choose to believe thoughts that are helpful and beneficial to your self-esteem.

Practice Self-Awareness

To do this, you first begin by practicing self-awareness. You need to be conscious and in tune with your thoughts to start challenging them. You also need to be patient with yourself and remind yourself that it takes time to change your thinking. Some ways to become more self-aware are:

Look at yourself objectively: When you are mindful of your thoughts, you can look at them objectively. This means you will see your thoughts for what they are and question them.

Write down your thoughts: Writing down your thoughts can help you see them more clearly. This is because it's hard to remember all of our thoughts, and when we write them down, we can look at them more objectively.

Create a plan or a list: Create an action plan for the goals or priorities you have for yourself or your family. This will help increase self-awareness, as you will be more focused on what you want to achieve rather than getting caught up in your thoughts. This can help you break down your thoughts, goals, or priorities into smaller, more manageable pieces. When we have a lot on our plates, it can be overwhelming, and this can lead to cognitive distortions.

Talk to someone you trust: Talking to someone you trust about your thoughts can be helpful because they can offer a different perspective and help you see your thoughts more clearly.

Self-reflection: This means you put aside time to contemplate your day or your thoughts. This can help you become more conscious of your thought processes, and it can help you see them more clearly.

Ask for feedback: Asking for feedback from others can offer a different perspective on how you think you feel or act and help you decipher your thoughts.

Cognitive distortions are just thoughts that are not helpful and dampen your self-esteem. They are not accurate. Changing our thoughts is not always easy. It takes practice.

But, it is possible. With time and effort, you and your child can learn to change cognitive distortions into more helpful thoughts.

MASTER YOUR THOUGHTS AND CHALLENGE THOUGHT DISTORTION

There are a few different ways you can master your thoughts. The first includes choosing what to focus on. You can focus on your child's strengths and positives rather than their weaknesses or negatives. If you are worried about your child's grades, you can focus on the fact that they are doing their best rather than the fact that they got a C on their math test.

You can also focus on your own strengths and positives. If you are worried about being a good parent, you can focus on the fact that you are loving and caring rather than on the fact that you sometimes lose your patience.

The second way to master your beliefs is to practice mindfulness. Instead of berating yourself over the past or worrying about the future, you can focus on the present moment. This can be accomplished by zeroing in on your breath or by focusing on your senses.

This can mean focusing on the sights and sounds around you or on the way your body feels. This will help you be more aware of the present moment, and it will help you let go of anxious thoughts about the past or future.

The third way to overcome your thoughts is to practice self-compassion. Practice kindness and understanding toward yourself, even when you make mistakes. It also means recognizing that everyone makes mistakes and that we all have flaws.

If you're worried about how you're doing as a parent, you can give yourself some self-compassion by saying, "I am doing my best, and I am a good person." This will help you feel better about yourself, and it will help you be more patient with your child.

If you're still anxious, you can try mastering your thoughts by focusing on a distraction. This means focusing on something other than the thing that is causing you anxiety. For example, if you are worried about your child's health, you can focus on something else, like a book you are reading or a project you are working on. This will rid your mind of your anxiety and help you relax.

Another option is to use action planning. This means breaking down the thing that is causing you anxiety into small, manageable steps. If your child's health is a concern, you can create an action plan. This could include buying healthy food for your family or ensuring your child gets exercise every day.

Action planning can prompt you to feel in charge and help you take the first steps toward solving the problem. Regardless of the method you choose, remember that change takes time. So be patient with yourself, and keep up the good work! Learning how to master your thoughts is an important part of child psychology. It can help you feel calmer and in control, and it can help you be a better parent.

Let's say you are aware of the cognitive distortion of all-or-nothing thinking. If you catch yourself thinking that your child is a failure because they got a C on a test, you can stop yourself and remind yourself that this is not helpful thinking.

You can also look for evidence that contradicts your thinking. If you think your child is a failure, you can remind yourself of all the times they have succeeded. By doing this, you can start to change your thinking and feel better about yourself and your child.

Self-Calming Techniques

Sometimes confronting thought distortions head-on or trying to reason with them can be ineffective or even make things worse. In these cases, it might be more helpful to use self-calming techniques to calm yourself down first. These are all about where you are allowing your thoughts to focus. By learning how to point your mind where you want it, it stops triggering anxiety through scary thoughts. Once you are calm, you can then deal with the thought distortions more effectively.

There are many ways to calm yourself down when you are feeling upset. Some people like to take a hot bath, listen to music, or read a book. Others might prefer to go for a walk, talk to a friend, or get some exercise.

Here are a few common ways you can practice self-calming:

Distract or Refocus Your Mind

When you are feeling anxious, it's helpful to find something else to focus on. This can be anything that distracts your mind from your anxieties, such as counting to 10 or 20. Or, you might try focusing on your breath and counting each inhale and exhale. You could concentrate on your breathing by pretending to blow bubbles.

You can also try to refocus your mind by thinking about something else. Try to picture the voice or face of someone close to you in your mind or think about a happy memory. You can visualize yourself in a peaceful place, like on the beach or in a meadow. Create a happy thought or a happy place for you to escape to.

Practice Self-Kindness

A healthy way to care for yourself is to be kind to yourself. Be gentle with yourself and speak to yourself in a loving way. For example, you might say, "I am doing the best I can," or "I am feeling really upset right now, and that's okay."

It can also be helpful to think about things you would say to a friend or loved one if they were in your situation. Would you be as critical of them as you are of yourself? Probably not. So, try to extend that same compassion to yourself.

Sit with Your Pet

Spending time with a pet can be very calming. If you have a pet, try sitting with them and stroking their fur. If you don't have a pet, you can try looking at pictures or videos of animals. There is something about the simple act of petting an animal that can be very soothing.

Plan an Activity

A great way to tame yourself is to do something you enjoy. This can be anything that makes you happy or you find relaxing. It might be listening to your favorite songs, reading a new book, going for a jog around your neighborhood, or taking a yoga class. Find something that works for you and that you can do when you are feeling upset.

Touch Something Comforting

Holding or touching something comforting can be beneficial in times of crisis. This might be a stuffed animal, a favorite blanket, or a piece of jewelry. Or, you might try hugging yourself. The act of physical touch can be very calming and help to ease anxiety.

Guided Imagery

Guided imagery is a relaxation technique that involves using your imagination to visualize a peaceful scene. This can be anything from a tropical beach to a meadow in the woods. Close your eyes and take a few deep breaths. Then, imagine the scene in as much detail as possible. Pay attention to what you see, smell, and feel. The more vivid the image, the more effective it will be.

List Positive Things

When you are feeling anxious or down, it's helpful to remind yourself of your positive attributes. Write down a list of qualities you have that you enjoy or think about times when you have felt proud of yourself. This can help boost your self-esteem and distract you from what is making you anxious. You can also list positive aspects of your life or the situation you're in, such as acknowledging aspects like "I have a roof over my head" or "I am loved."

5–4–3–2–1

This is a mindfulness technique that can help you focus on the present moment and ease anxiety. To do this, simply name 5 things you see around you, 4 things you feel, 3 things you hear, 2 things you smell, and 1 thing you taste. This can ground you in the present moment and take your mind off of whatever is causing you stress.

Self-Soothing Objects

Some people find it helpful to carry around a small object they can use for self-soothing. This might be a stone, a piece of jewelry, or a small toy. Worry beads, fidget spinners, or other tactile objects are great for self-soothing. You can even carry around a photo of someone or something that provides you with joy. When you are feeling anxious or upset, you can hold on to the object and focus on its texture or color to ease your anxiety and make you feel calmer.

Slow Down Your Breathing

When you are feeling anxious, you may struggle with your breathing as it becomes shallow and rapid, like you ran a marathon. This can make you feel even more anxious. To counter this, try to take slow, deep breaths. Inhale through your nose, counting to four. Then exhale through your mouth, counting to four. Repeat this several times. This will help to slow down your breathing and ease your anxiety.

Drink Water

Sometimes, anxiety can be caused by dehydration. Drink a glass of water or herbal tea to help you relax. Chamomile tea is especially helpful for anxiety.

Square or Box Breathing

This breathing exercise can help ease anxiety. Start by inhaling for four counts. Hold your breath for four counts. Then exhale for four counts. Hold your breath for four counts. Repeat this several times.

Belly Breathing

This breathing exercise can help ease our nerves. Place one hand on your stomach and the other on your chest. Slowly inhale through your nose, letting your stomach expand. Then exhale through your mouth, letting your stomach fall. Repeat this several times.

Swim or Spend Time in Nature

Spending time in nature can help to ease anxiety. Go for a walk in the park, lie on the grass, or go swimming in a lake. This will help you relax and feel more connected to the world around you.

Meditate

Meditation is when you focus your attention and clear your mind of thoughts so you can feel calm and centered. To meditate, find a quiet place to sit or lie down. Close your eyes and focus on your breath. Inhale slowly and deeply, then exhale slowly. Continue this for several minutes. You can also focus on a mantra, which is a particular word or positive phrase that you repeat to yourself.

Self-Soothing Mantras

Some people find it helpful to use mantras for self-soothing. A mantra is a word or a positive sentence you repeat to yourself. By focusing on something positive, you can ease anxiety and focus your attention on something positive. Some mantras you can use for self-soothing are: "I am safe," "I am loved," or "I am enough."

Exercise

Exercise can help to release endorphins, which have mood-boosting effects. A moderate amount of exercise is the best for anxiety relief. You don't have to go to the gym or go for a run. Even a brisk walk can help. Other exercises you can do are yoga, dancing, spinning, tai chi, and qigong.

There are many ways to deal with anxiety. Some people find that one method works better for them, while others have to try a few different things before they find what works. Not to mention, what works for you might not work for your children. Experiment with various techniques and determine what works best for you. Remember, everyone experiences anxiety differently, so what works for others may not work for you and your children. Be patient and keep trying different things until you find what helps you to ease your anxiety.

Play Mental-Focused or Self-Control Games

Games that focus on mental skills or self-control can help your child to develop the ability to regulate their emotions. These games can also help to increase their focus and attention. Examples of games you can play with your child are:

- Catch Your Breath

In this game, you take deep breaths together and see who can blow the biggest bubbles.

- The Balloon Game

In this game, you try to keep a balloon in the air for as long as possible.

- I Spy

This game increases your child's focus and attention.

- Simon Says

This game develops your child's ability to follow instructions.

- Red Light, Green Light

This game enhances your child's ability to regulate their emotions.

- The Squiggle Game

In this game, you draw a squiggle on a piece of paper and see how many things you can turn it into. This game can help your child be creative and express themselves in an unpredictable yet safe way.

- Memory Games

Memory games help to improve your child's memory and attention.

- Waiting Games

Games that focus on waiting patiently can help your child learn to regulate their emotions.

RESPOND, DON'T REACT

When feeling anxious, responding to the anxiety rather than reacting to it is important. A reaction is an automatic, emotional response to a situation. A reaction is usually negative and can make anxiety worse. For example, if you have a fear of flying, you might have a reaction to wanting to get off the plane as soon as possible. This would make your anxiety worse and could even lead to a panic attack.

A response is a more deliberate, thought-out action. A response is usually positive and can help to ease anxiety. If you're fearful of spiders, you might respond by doing some deep-breathing exercises and listening to relaxation music. This would help to ease your anxiety and make the situation more bearable.

When we enter the fight-or-flight stage, our higher thinking shuts down and we cannot problem-solve well or make moral decisions. Therefore, responding first will prompt you to stay relaxed and make more rational decisions.

Responding is to take a step back rather than reacting emotionally to the situation. For example, if you are in a meeting and you start to feel anxious, rather than getting up and leaving the room, you might take a few deep, calming breaths and remind yourself that you can handle this. You will feel more relaxed and make the best decision for you.

Other ways you can prepare for anxieties are:

- Plan and practice

Plan ahead for situations that might make you anxious. You think about what you will do and how you will react. This can help to ease anxiety because you will know what to expect, and you will have a plan to follow. Practicing your response will make you more likely to react how you want to.

- Change your perspective

Look at the situation differently. For example, if you are anxious about flying, you might tell yourself that it is just a plane and that there is nothing to be afraid of. By changing the way you look at the situation, you can experience less anxiety.

- Acknowledge the facts

Accept the situation for what it is. For example, if you are anxious about flying, you might acknowledge that the chance of the plane crashing is minor. By facing the situation head-on, you can ease your nerves.

- Use your hindsight

Look back on the situation after it has happened. For example, if you are nervous around large animals, you can reflect on the experience and remind yourself that you're still okay, which can ease your nerves because you can see the situation is not as terrible as you believed it was.

Other helpful ways to respond to anxiety are:

- Take a few deep breaths.
- Tell yourself that you can handle this.
- Focus on the present moment.
- Use positive self-talk.
- Challenge your negative thoughts.
- Visualize a calm place.

Responding instead of reacting is also an important practice to use with our children. It's difficult to do this when we are feeling anxious, but it is so important. Instead of reacting when they do something wrong or something you don't like, take a step back and respond to help them learn and grow.

For example, if your child throws a tantrum, you might respond by helping them to calm down and then talking to them about what they are feeling. This will help them understand their emotions and how to deal with them constructively. Modeling this behavior for our children will help them learn how to deal with anxiety in a more constructive way.

When our children are feeling anxious, we can help them by:

- Encouraging them to take deep breaths.
- Helping them to identify their thoughts and feelings.
- Teaching them how to use positive self-talk.
- helping them to come up with a plan for dealing with their anxiety
- Encouraging them to practice their plan.
- Helping them to reflect on their progress.

Anxiety is a normal and healthy emotion. It becomes a problem when it interferes with our lives. By responding instead of reacting and teaching our children to do the same, we can learn to be less anxious.

AVOID BLAMING

The blame culture is alive and well in many families. This is when parents blame their children for everything that goes wrong. Blaming is when you hold someone responsible for something that isn't their fault. It's a way of assigning responsibility to someone without evidence. This can lead to feelings of shame, guilt, and low self-esteem. It can also induce behavioral problems. Blaming culture can create a toxic environment, so it's best to avoid it.

How to Stop Blaming

If you constantly assign blame, there are some things you can do to stop.

First, try to notice when you're doing it. This can be difficult because we often do it without realizing it. Pay attention to your thoughts and feelings in stressful situations. If you're blaming someone, stop, and take a step back.

Understand the reasons you blame others. Are you trying to make yourself feel better? Are you trying to avoid taking responsibility? Once you understand the "why" behind your actions, you can work on changing your behavior.

Then try to reframe the situation. Instead of blaming someone, try to understand what happened and why. This can be difficult but remember that people are not always responsible for their actions. Sometimes things just happen.

Become more compassionate. Instead of judging someone, try to understand them. Everyone makes mistakes. Try to see the situation from their perspective. Change your mindset to understand that we are still growing and learning. No one is perfect.

Additionally, focus on what you can change. You can't control or supervise what other people do, but you can manage your own actions. Choose to respond in a way that is helpful, not harmful.

Take responsibility for your own happiness. Don't wait for someone else to make you happy. You create and maintain your own happiness. Choose to do things that make you happy. Determine which activities you enjoy and do them every day.

Finally, try to let go of the need to control. When we're constantly blaming others, we're actually trying to control the situation. We want to predict and control what happens. But life is unpredictable. Things will happen that are out of our control. The best we can do is to be prepared and to deal with them the best way we can.

With your child, you can stop the blame culture by:

- Not blaming your children for everything.
- Talking to them when they make mistakes and helping them learn how to do better next time.
- Being a role model by not blaming others yourself.
- Taking responsibility for your own happiness.
- Focusing on what you can change.
- Letting go of the need to control.

Blaming others is easy, but it's not helpful. Instead, focus on what you can change. You can't control other people, but you can control your own actions. Choose to act or respond in a way that promotes more positivity and less harm. Be more compassionate and understanding. And most importantly, take responsibility for your own happiness.

It takes time and effort to change your mindset, but it's worth it. You'll be happier and more stress-free. And your child will benefit from your positive example.

SELF-CALMING PRACTICES

For the next week, engage in at least one self-calming activity that you can do with your child(ren) each day.

Examples:

- Deep breathing
- Yoga
- Mindfulness meditation
- Progressive muscle relaxation
- Guided imagery
- Art
- Music
- Reading
- Organizing
- Crafting
- Gardening
- Hiking

Take some time for yourself each day to do something you enjoy which will not produce stress and anxiety. Then reflect on your experiences together. However, life doesn't become calmer only because you do. You can also address other areas in your life to make them more relaxing. So, how can you create a calm family environment?

5

CHAOS TO CALM

I've learned through the years that it's not where you live,
it's the people who surround you that make you feel at home.

— J.B. MCGEE

It's been said that home is where the heart is. And while that may be true, it's also important to remember that home is where we raise our families. It's a place of love, security, and comfort. But it can also be a place of chaos.

With work, school, extracurricular activities, and family obligations, it's easy for our homes to become chaotic. But when our homes are chaotic, it can lead to stress and anxiety.

CREATING A CALMING FAMILY ENVIRONMENT

A calming family environment is one that is nurturing, supportive, and safe. It's a place where everyone feels valued and respected. And it's a place where we can go to relax and rejuvenate. Without it, we can feel lost and alone.

There are many ways to create a calming family environment. Let's start with some basics.

Declutter the Home

One of the quickest and easiest ways to reduce stress is to declutter the home. When our homes are cluttered, it can feel like our lives are out of control. But when we declutter, we take back control.

Here are some tips for decluttering:

- Start with one room at a time.
- Focus on one area at a time.
- Set a timer for 15 minutes and declutter as much as you can in that time.
- Donate or sell items that you no longer need or want.
- Recycle anything that can't be donated or sold.

The floor should be clutter-free so housemates and guests can walk around freely and safely. There should also be a place for everything so that it's easy to find what you need when you need it. Creating designated spaces for certain items or activities can help to keep the home more organized and less chaotic.

Create Child-Friendly Spaces

Children need a place to call their own where they can play, learn, and explore. This can be their bedroom, a playroom, or even a corner of the living room. Create a child-friendly space that is safe and inviting.

Here are some tips for creating child-friendly spaces:

- Make sure there is enough room, and it is uncluttered for the child to move around freely.
- Remove any sharp or breakable objects.
- Make sure all toys and furniture are age appropriate.
- Encourage creativity by providing art supplies and other materials.

Create a Peaceful Space

Every home should have a peaceful space where family members can go to relax and rejuvenate. This can be a corner of the room, a cozy chair, or even outside in the backyard. Keep a space readily available that is free of clutter and distractions. This should be a place where we can go to take a break from the chaos of everyday life.

Some ideas for creating a peaceful space:

- Add some cozy blankets and pillows.
- Place a few candles around the room.
- Diffuse some essential oils.
- Play some calming music.
- Add some fresh flowers or plants.

Have Everyone Help with Chores

Another way to reduce stress is to have everyone help with chores. When we all pitch in, it can help to lighten the load and make the home more organized and less chaotic.

Some ideas for involving everyone in chores:

- Create a chore chart or list.
- Assign specific tasks to each family member.
- Rotate tasks on a weekly or monthly basis.
- Set a timer and see how quickly everyone can complete their chores.
- Give everyone a break once the chores are done.

Organize Your Belongings

Organizing your belongings can also help to reduce stress and anxiety. When we know where everything is, it's one less thing to worry about. And when our homes are organized, it can help us feel more in control.

Here are some tips for organizing your belongings:

- Use storage baskets, bins, and containers.
- Label everything, so it's easy to find.
- Recycle anything that can't be donated or sold.
- Keep only what you use on a regular basis.
- Think vertically if you run out of storage space (shelves, hooks, etc.).

Beware of Sensory Issues

Some people, children especially, are sensitive to certain sounds, smells, and textures. This can make it difficult to relax or concentrate. If anyone in your house has sensory issues, it's important to be conscious of those concerns so you can steer clear of anything that might trigger a reaction.

Some ideas for avoiding sensory triggers:

- Wear noise-canceling headphones.
- Use a diffuser for essential oils.
- Wash bedding in scent-free laundry detergent.
- Avoid potent smells or perfumes.
- Wear soft, comfortable clothing.
- Choose fabrics that aren't scratchy or irritating.

Creating a calm and relaxed home environment is essential for the well-being of the entire family. By decluttering and creating child-friendly spaces, we can reduce stress and anxiety and create a more peaceful home.

Bring Nature Inside

Another way to create a calm and relaxing environment is to bring nature inside. Studies have shown that being around plants can help to reduce stress and anxiety. And just looking at pictures of nature has been shown to lower blood pressure and heart rate.

Some ideas for bringing nature inside:

- Place a few potted plants around the house.
- Put a fish tank in the living room or bedroom.
- Hang some pictures or paintings of nature scenes.
- Keep a bowl of fresh fruit on the kitchen counter.
- Display flowers in vases around the house.

Purge Your Belongings

We often hold on to things that we no longer need or want. But these items can take up valuable space in our homes and contribute to the feeling of being overwhelmed.

To declutter your belongings, start by going through each room and getting rid of anything you no longer need or want. Donate items that are in good condition and recycle or trash anything that is damaged or broken.

Creating a calm and stress-free home environment takes some effort, but it's worth it. When we declutter, have everyone help with chores, and create child-friendly spaces, we can reduce our anxieties and create a more relaxing environment.

Family Rituals and Traditions

Another way to create a calm family environment is to establish family rituals. Family rituals are activities we do together regularly. They can be as simple as having a family dinner every night or taking a walk together after dinner.

These rituals give us a sense of belonging and help to create strong bonds between family members. They can also provide a much-needed sense of stability in our lives.

Some ideas for family rituals:

- Have a family dinner together every night.
- Take a walk together after dinner.
- Play games together on the weekends.
- Have a picnic in the park once a month.
- Plant a garden together in the spring.

Developing positive family rituals and traditions can help to create a calm and relaxing environment for the entire family. These activities help to reduce stress and anxiety, which can create a more peaceful vibe in your home.

Reduce Screen Time

Spending too much time on screens can lead to stress and anxiety. It can also make it difficult to focus and be productive. So, limit screen time and take breaks throughout the day.

Some ideas for reducing screen time:

- Set a daily limit for screen time.
- Take regular breaks throughout the day.
- Do something else when you're feeling bored or restless.

- Turn off electronics an hour before bedtime.

Limiting screen time is important for reducing stress and anxiety. It's also important for our mental and physical health. So, take a break from your screens and enjoy the world around you.

Family Meetings

Family meetings are a great way to communicate and connect with family members. They provide an opportunity for everyone to share their thoughts, feelings, and ideas. Family meetings can be held weekly, biweekly, or monthly. They can be informal or structured. And they can last for any amount of time.

The most important thing is that everyone participates.

Some tips for holding a successful family meeting:

- Pick a day and time that works for everyone.
- Make sure the meeting is focused and organized.
- Encourage everyone to participate.
- Listen to what everyone has to say.
- Respect different opinions.
- End on a positive note.

By holding regular family meetings, we can create a calm and stress-free environment for the entire family. Keep an open mind and encourage your family, children included, to release their pent-up emotions or thoughts.

Do Activities Together Often

Doing activities together as a family can help to create a sense of unity and connection. It can also be a lot of fun and a great way to bond with each other!

Some ideas for activities you can do together:

- Bake cookies or cakes.
- Play tag or hide-and-seek.
- Have a water balloon fight.
- Make homemade pizzas.
- Plant a garden.
- Go on a nature walk.
- Ride bikes together.

Set Ground Rules

Set some rules for the family to help create a calmer and more orderly environment. These rules can be as simple as no yelling, no hitting, and no name-calling. Or they can be more specific, like no TV during dinner, no cell phones at the table, and no screens in the bedroom.

Whatever rules you decide to set, make sure everyone understands them and agrees with them. And be sure to enforce the rules consistently.

Setting rules is a great way to help reduce stress and create a calmer and more orderly environment. By setting and enforcing rules, we can help to create a more peaceful home for everyone.

Encourage Downtime

Everyone should have some time to relax and unwind. This is especially true for kids. After a long day at school or after playing with friends, they need some time for themselves.

Some ideas for encouraging downtime:

- Set a regular bedtime and stick to it.
- Turn off electronics an hour before bedtime.
- Read a book or listen to music before bedtime.
- Create a calm and relaxing bedroom environment.

Encouraging downtime is important for reducing stress and promoting relaxation. It also improves our mental and physical well-being.

Create Routines

Routines can help to structure our days and make us feel more in control. When our lives are chaotic, routine can be a lifesaver. It can also provide comfort and a sense of predictability, which is especially helpful for children who struggle with anxiety.

Some ideas for routines:

- Wake up at the same time each day.
- Create a morning routine to help set the tone for the day.
- Eat regular meals.
- Exercise at the same time each day.

- Spend time with family and friends.
- Include regular self-soothing techniques like yoga, meditation, or journaling.
- Go to bed at the same time each day.
- Create an evening routine that helps you unwind and prepare for the following day.

Creating a routine can help you and your family focus on what's essential while also relieving stress with its predictability. So, if you're feeling overwhelmed, take some time to create routines.

We can feel more in control with the help of healthy habits. When our lives are chaotic, healthy habits can be a lifesaver. Since habits give your child a sense of predictability, they might find comfort in these routines and struggle with anxiety less.

Creating healthy family habits is a great way to focus on what's truly important together while also reducing stress. So, if you're feeling anxious, take time to incorporate healthy family habits into your routine.

Talk about Feelings a Lot

Families who talk about their feelings a lot are more mentally healthy because speaking about your troubles helps build trust and foster communication. If you're uncomfortable sharing your feelings with your family, you can journal or talk to others, but ensure you encourage your child to also talk about their feelings.

Talking about your feelings is a great way to reduce stress and promote mental health. It's also a great way to build trust and foster communication. Also, teach your children how to talk and express their feelings. It's an important skill that will help them throughout their lives. You can teach them how to name and label their feelings (angry, sad, happy, anxious, calm, etc.).

Then, you can help them understand and express their feelings healthily, which is a critical skill that will help them well into their adult lives. They can do this by talking about how they feel, writing about their feelings, or talking to a therapist. You can also include other coping strategies, like yoga, meditation, or journaling.

Provide Positive Reinforcement

Positive reinforcement involves providing rewards for desired behaviors. This can help to increase the behaviors you want and decrease the poor behaviors.

Some ways to provide positive reinforcement:

- Praise your child when they display desired behaviors.
- Offer rewards for desired behaviors.
- Ignore undesired behaviors.

Be the Example

Be the example you want for your children. This means modeling the desired behaviors yourself. If you want your children to eat healthy, then you should eat healthy. You should exercise if you want your children to exercise. Be kind if you want your children to be kind. Children learn by example, so it's important to set a good one.

Some ways to set a good example:

- Model the desired behaviors yourself.
- Explain why you're doing the desired behaviors.
- Encourage your children to do the same.

You can teach your children by modeling the desired behaviors yourself, explaining why you're doing them, and encouraging your children to do the same.

Talk to Children in Ways They Understand

Talk to children in ways they understand. This means using language to which they can relate. It also means avoiding technical jargon. Instead, focus on explaining things in simple terms. This will help children to understand and feel more comfortable.

Some ways to talk to children in ways they understand:

- Lower to their eye level

- Get down on their level when you talk to them.
- Make eye contact.
- Use simple words and phrases.

- Use relatable content

  - Use examples they can relate to.
  - Make connections to their interests.
  - Explain things in simple terms.

- Offer genuine and encouraging compliments

  - Be sincere.
  - Encourage their efforts.
  - Make them feel good about themselves.

- Ask open-ended questions
- Ask about them, their day, and their thoughts

  - Make conversation.
  - Ask questions about their day.

- Show that you care about them
- Pay attention to their body language and nonverbal cues

  - Observe their body language.
  - Listen to their tone of voice.

  ○ Read their facial expressions.

- Don't interrupt

  ○ Listen to understand, not offer solutions.

- Speak in a serious tone

  ○ Don't raise your voice when disciplining them.

- Simplify lectures

  ○ Offer options that are suitable to you but still give them a sense of control.

  - Welcome their questions
  - Leave time for them to process information

Help Your Child Face Their Fears Gently

Helping your child face their fears can be a laborious task. You want to encourage them to confront their fears, but you don't want to push them too hard. It's important to find a balance between the two. Here are some tips to help you:

Build Gradually

When you're helping your child face their fears, build up to their worst fear slowly. If you try to push them too hard, they may become overwhelmed and give up. Start with small steps and work your way up. Start with the smallest, simplest, least scary idea of their fear. For example, if they are afraid of dogs, you could start with a picture of a silly or happy dog.

Then progress to watching movies or playing games with a friendly dog. When the child feels ready, allow them to touch a real dog (that you know is well trained and safe) for a few seconds. Slowly increase the time and repeat each level until the child feels absolutely no fear at that level. Always stick to what feels comfortable for the child.

Follow Your Child's Pace

Let your child set the pace when they're challenging their fears. If they're not ready to confront their fears yet, pushing them will only make things worse. Wait until they're ready, and then help them take the next step.

Encourage Them

Letting them know you're there for them and believing in them can make a big difference.

Don't Include Negative Reinforcement

When you're prompting your child to face their fears, avoid negative reinforcement. This includes things like threats, ultimatums, and punishment. These things will only make the situation worse, and they'll cause your child to resent you.

Be Patient and Persistent

Assisting your child when they are challenging their anxieties can be a difficult and slow process. Be patient and persevere through the tough times. Remember that you're doing this for your child and that it's all worth it in the end. Keep pushing them gently and, eventually, they'll make progress.

Practice Empathy

Practice empathy when you're helping your child with exposure therapy. Empathy is being understanding and sharing the feelings that someone else experiences. Put yourself in their position and try to understand how they're feeling.

This will help you be more understanding and patient with them.

Give Your Child Freedom

When you're prompting your child to challenge themselves, let them have freedom. This means you shouldn't force them to do anything. Instead, let them make their own decisions and choices. This will help them feel in control and give them the confidence to face their fears.

Prompt Them to Talk about Their Fears

One of the best ways to help your child face their fears is to prompt them to talk about their fears. This will help them understand and process their fears. It will also help you understand their fears and how best to help them.

Validate Their Fears

When your child shares their fears, validate their emotions or experiences. This means you should acknowledge that their fears are real and they're allowed to feel afraid. This will help them feel seen and heard. It will also help them know that their fears are valid and that you understand them.

Make a Plan Together

Once you've talked about their fears, it's time to make a plan together. This will help them feel empowered and in control. It will also help to ensure they're comfortable with the plan and understand it. Put support systems in place for if and when the trigger arises. For instance, consider what you can do or teach your child to do that will help them deal with anxiety or lessen it.

Or you could create a plan for when your child sees a dog running loose somewhere. Or you could let your child carry a stick or safety device in places where dogs could be an issue. Another option would be to take them to dog safety training lessons (only if they are ready for that) or ask your friends and family to put their dogs away when you visit.

Teach Your Child(ren) How to Manage Their Anxiety Better

Being equipped with the proper tools to manage their anxiety can be very helpful. Just remember that each child is different and will require a different approach and plan. The most important thing is to be there for them, to listen, and to understand. Here are a few suggestions:

Breathing Exercises

Breathing exercises can prompt your child to calm down and relax. There are many breathing exercises you can do with your child. Here are a few examples:

- 4–7–8 breathing exercise

In this exercise, you breathe in for 4 seconds, hold your breath for 7 seconds, and then breathe out for 8 seconds.

- Belly breathing

In this exercise, you place your hand on your stomach and focus on breathing into your hand.

- Blowing bubbles

In this exercise, you blow bubbles and focus on taking deep breaths.

- Pinwheels

In this exercise, you make a pinwheel and focus on blowing it.

Meditate Together

Meditation can help your child to focus and calm their mind. It can also help to increase their ability to regulate their emotions. There are several types of meditation you can do with your child. Here are a few examples:

- Body scan meditation

In this exercise, you focus on each part of your body and on relaxing your muscles.

- Guided meditation

In this exercise, you follow along with a guided meditation.

- Mindfulness meditation

In this exercise, you focus on the present moment and on your breath.

- Visualization meditation

In this exercise, you focus on relaxing and visualizing a peaceful place.

- Progressive muscle relaxation

In this exercise, you focus on tensing and relaxing each muscle group in your body.

- Yoga

Yoga can promote more calming and relaxing feelings within your child. Yoga can also help to increase their flexibility and strength.

Teach Them How to Recognize Their Fears

Identifying your child's fears is crucial to success because it will help them better understand and manage their anxiety. Here are some tips:

- Talk to your child about their fears and ask them to describe what they feel.
- Help them label their feelings by teaching them words such as scared, worried, or anxious.
- Encourage them to talk about their fears with you or another trusted adult.

When explaining fears and other emotions, you can:

- Use authentic examples: "I was afraid of the dark when I was your age. It felt like there were monsters in my closet."

- Listen to your child and validate their feelings: "It sounds like you're terrified of dogs. That can be really scary."
- Help them understand that it is normal to feel scared sometimes and that everyone has fears.

When your child can recognize their fears, they can work on managing them.

Create a Safe Space Full of Stimulating Activities

A safe space is a place where your child can go to relax and feel in control. This can be a specific room in your house or a corner in their bedroom. The space should be full of things that make them feel happy and calm. You can also consider creating stimulating sensory activities. Here are some ideas:

Visual: Fill the space with their favorite colors, pictures of loved ones, or calming scenery.

Auditory: Play calming music or white noise in the space.

Tactile: Fill the space with soft blankets, stuffed animals, or stress balls.

Smell: Diffuse calming essential oils such as lavender or chamomile.

Taste: Have healthy snacks available, such as fruits and vegetables, yogurt, or whole-grain crackers.

Movement: Have toys and games available that they can move around with, such as a jump rope, hula hoop, or balls.

Create a calm-down box: This is a box that is filled with things that help your child to calm down. Some ideas for the box are:

- Stuffed animals
- Picture of a loved one
- A favorite book
- A worry stone
- Coloring books and crayons
- Bubbles
- A small toy

Involve your child in creating the box and let them choose what goes inside. This will help them feel more in control, and they can pick items that suit them the best.

Create a sensory bottle: This is a bottle that is filled with different materials, such as water, glitter, and food coloring. It can help to calm your child by providing them with a visual to focus on. It is also an awesome way for them to learn about different textures and colors.

Here is a recipe for a simple sensory bottle:

- 1/2 cup of hot water
- 1/2 cup of glitter
- A few drops of food coloring

- 1/2 cup of clear glue
- A clean plastic bottle with a lid

Instructions:

1. Add the hot water, glitter, and food coloring to the bottle.
2. Add the glue and screw on the lid.
3. Shake the bottle until the glitter is dispersed.
4. Let the bottle sit for 24 hours before use.

Your child can use the sensory bottle when they are feeling anxious or stressed. They can shake it, turn it upside down, and watch the glitter fall.

Teach Them to Ask for Help

A healthy way to educate your child on how to communicate appropriately is to teach them how to ask for help. This will help them feel more in control and less anxious. Here are some tips:

- Teach them who they can go to for help. This could be a parent, teacher, or another trusted adult.
- Help them practice asking for help. You can role-play with them or have them practice on a stuffed animal.
- Encourage them to speak up when they are feeling anxious or scared.

- Reward them when they ask for help. This could be a special treat or some extra attention.
- Let them know it is okay to feel scared sometimes and that everyone needs help sometimes.

Anxiety can be a tough challenge for children to deal with. However, by teaching them how to manage their anxiety, you can help them feel more positive about their abilities and less afraid of their fears.

Teach Children How to Ask for Help

Asking for help can feel like an embarrassing thing to do, but it's an important skill for children to learn. Help your child(ren) understand that it's okay to ask for help and that everyone needs help sometimes. This will prompt them to feel more comfortable asking for help when they need it. They shouldn't feel ashamed or feel they should apologize when they need assistance.

If you're one to shy away from asking for help, this can reflect on your children. Start by realizing your own attitudes and behaviors toward asking for help. Children often model their behavior after their parents, so it's important to set a good example.

Here are a few things to consider:

- Self-criticism

Avoid being too critical of yourself when you make a mistake. We are our own worst enemies, and we might stop ourselves from seeking help because we think it makes us look weak or ignorant.

- Shame

Don't feel ashamed to ask for help. Everyone needs help sometimes.

- Vulnerability

Realize that asking for help doesn't make you vulnerable. It actually strengthens you. It shows you're willing to admit you need assistance and are open to learning.

- Negative associations

Try to change your mindset about asking for help. Instead of thinking of it as a bad thing, think of it as an opportunity to grow and learn. You are not lazy or pathetic for asking for help; you are taking charge of your life and taking steps to improve your situation.

- Let go of perceptions

Often, we have a set idea of how we should be, and asking for help goes against that. We think we should be able to do everything on our own, but that's not realistic. It's okay to ask for help. It doesn't make you any less capable.

- Self-sacrificing beliefs

We often put others before ourselves, but that shouldn't be the case. Asking for help is not selfish. It's actually quite self-less. It shows you're willing to do what's best for yourself and others.

- Stop overestimating rejection

We tend to think that people will judge us or think less of us if we ask for help, but that's usually not the case. Most people are more than happy to help, so don't let your fears get in the way.

Helping your child(ren) to understand these things can go a long way in teaching them how to ask for help. Here are a few tips:

- Talk about how everyone needs help sometimes.
- Explain that it's okay to ask for help.
- Encourage them to ask for help when they need it.
- Don't berate yourself when you make a mistake.

- Help them see that mistakes are opportunities to learn.
- Change your mindset about asking for help.
- Don't be afraid to ask for help.
- Show them that asking for help is not selfish.
- Explain that people are usually happy to help.
- Encourage them to be open and honest about their feelings.

Additionally, here are phrases you can use when you need help and that you can teach to your child(ren):

- Can you help me with this?
- I'm not sure how to do this. Can you help me?
- Can you explain this to me?
- I'm feeling overwhelmed. Can you help me?
- I need some assistance. Can you help me?
- Thank you for your help.
- I appreciate your help.
- Thank you for taking the time to help me.
- I need help with this.
- Sometimes I also need help.
- It's okay to ask for help.
- Let's find someone who can help us with this.
- Asking for help is not a sign of weakness; it's a sign of strength.
- There's no shame in asking for help.
- It's okay not to know everything.

- Nobody knows everything, and that's why we ask for help.
- It's better to ask for help than to struggle on your own.

Helping children to understand how and when to ask for help can be very helpful. It can teach them to be independent and to take charge of their own lives. Asking for help is a strength, not a sign of being fragile. When you ask for help, it shows you're open to learning and willing to accept the knowledge others have. So don't be afraid to ask for help. It's the first step to taking charge of your life.

TEACHING THROUGH PLAY

Games are an easy and fun way to educate children about emotions. They're also great for connecting with your child and having fun. When playing games with your child, try to focus on games involving emotions. This will help your child to learn about different emotions and how to express them. It will also help them have fun.

If you decide to teach your children through playtime, here are some tips:

Play Pretend

Playing pretend is an awesome way to teach children through interactions. It's also a lot of fun. When you're playing pretend, try to make the emotions as realistic as possible. This will help your child understand the emotions and also keep them interested in the game.

Complete a Project

Doing a project together is an awesome way to spend some quality time with your child while sneaking in some education about emotions. When you're doing a project, try to focus on emotions. They can create an art piece that reflects how they're feeling or a specific emotion in general. Allow them to convey themselves how they see fit.

Play Music and Sing

Music is a creative and fun way to educate your child about how they feel and why. When playing music, try to focus on songs that involve emotions. They can act and sing along, which will keep them engaged as they learn.

Some wonderful songs to play for your child about emotions are:

- "If You're Happy and You Know It"
- "The Wheels on the Bus"
- "Row, Row, Row Your Boat"
- "I'm a Little Teapot"

Play Sports

Playing sports can be an awesome opportunity to teach your child about emotions or how to release them in a healthy way. It can also be a substantial form of quality time. You can use this time to talk about how they're feeling or just to let them blow off some steam.

Invite Them When You Run Errands

Including your child in your errands is a great way to teach them about emotions and introduce them to real-world experiences. It also prompts some alone time with your children. When you're running errands, explain to them in rich detail what you are doing and why. This will help your child be more observant and also keep them engaged in the errand.

Ask for Help

Children have a natural inclination to want to help. Asking for their help is a great way to share responsibilities and foster their sense of ownership. It's also a great way to teach them about emotions. When you're asking for help, be specific about what you need help with. This will help your child to understand the task and focus on helping you. The more they help now, the better they'll be at accomplishing their own responsibilities in the future.

However, as much as we as parents aim to do everything we can for our children and assist them in their time of need, sometimes a child's anxiety and fear require next-level help.

A QUICK NOTE!

If you are enjoying this book so far, I would appreciate it if you left a short review on Amazon. It is free and shouldn't take longer than 60 seconds.

As an independent author and publisher with a small marketing budget, reviews are my livelihood on this platform.

You can leave your honest feedback by clicking on the link below or scanning the QR code:

https://is.gd/3yxmos

I love hearing from my readers, and I personally read every single review.

Thank you for your time.

Sincerely,

Lulu James

P.S. If you'd like to know when my next book comes out and want to receive occasional updates, please email me at

lulujames@lighttightstory.com.

6

PROFESSIONAL HELP

Making fears known, and bringing them into the light, takes their power over you away. Facing our fears and anxiety is a tough challenge but doing so is an important first step in managing them. In this chapter, we're going to talk about some professional help that's available for children who are struggling with anxiety. We'll also go over some things to keep in mind when seeking treatment.

CHOOSING THE RIGHT THERAPIST

When looking for someone to help your child, search for a therapist with whom your child feels comfortable. It's also important to search for a therapist who is qualified and has experience working with children with anxiety. Here are some questions to ask when looking for a therapist:

- What is their experience in treating children with anxiety?
- What credentials do they have?
- Do they have any specialized training in treating anxiety?
- What is their treatment approach?
- Do they use evidence-based treatments?

- Do they have experience working with children with my child's specific anxiety disorder?
- Do they have any reviews or references? What do they say?
- How long will treatment last?
- What is the frequency of sessions?
- How much will the treatment cost?
- What are their office hours?
- Do they offer any sliding scale fee options?
- What is their cancellation policy?
- Do they have any payment plans available?
- Do they accept health insurance?

Once you've found a therapist you're comfortable with, the next step is scheduling an initial consultation. This meeting will occur among you, your child, and the therapist to see if treatment is the right fit. It's also an opportunity for you to ask questions you may have about the therapist's qualifications, experience, or treatment approach.

WHAT TO EXPECT FROM EXPOSURE THERAPY

The first few therapy sessions will focus on getting to know your child and their unique experiences with anxiety. There might be questionnaires or forms to fill out for the first meetings. Before the healing process can start, an analysis may also be included to help the therapist understand what will work best for your child. The therapist will also want to talk to you and your child about your goals for treatment. Be honest and open with the therapist about what you hope to achieve through therapy. They may also want to get to know the family and understand the home environment.

The therapist will probably ask about your child's medical history, family history, and current stressors. They'll also ask about your child's anxiety symptoms, how long they've been experiencing them, and how they're affecting your child's life.

Once the therapist has gathered this information, they'll work with you and your child to develop a treatment plan. This plan will likely include weekly sessions, as well as some things to do at home in between sessions. The therapist may also recommend some changes to the home environment, such as setting limits on screen time or establishing a bedtime routine.

After the initial meetings, the therapist will teach your child coping and problem-solving skills. They'll also help them identify and challenge their negative thoughts and beliefs about anxiety. As your child feels more comfortable and confident, the therapist will help them to gradually face their fears in a safe and controlled way. This process is called exposure therapy. Treatment typically lasts 8–10 weeks, although some children may need more or less time depending on the severity of their anxiety.

As your child starts to make progress in therapy, the therapist will help you learn how to support your child at home. They'll also provide guidance on how to deal with any setbacks or relapses. With time and support, most children can overcome their anxiety and live happy and fulfilling lives.

If you think your child might benefit from therapy, don't hesitate to reach out for help. Early intervention is crucial for preventing anxiety from becoming a more serious problem.

DURING A SESSION

During exposure therapy sessions, your child will work with the therapist to determine and reframe their negative emotions or beliefs about anxiety. The therapist will also expose them gradually to their fears. This process is called exposure therapy.

Therapy sessions typically last 50–60 minutes. The number of sessions will depend on the severity of your child's anxiety and their goals for treatment. Most children see a therapist weekly for 8–10 weeks, although some may need more or less time depending on their progress.

As a parent, you may not always be in the room during a session with your child. Generally, this depends on your child's age and the treatment plan. However, this is normal, and it gives your child the chance to talk openly with the therapist about their anxiety. In order to build trust, the therapist will probably ask your permission to speak with your child without you being in the room. The therapist may also want to meet with you separately to get your input and feedback.

You can expect the therapist to provide you with support and guidance between sessions. They may also give you some things to do at home to help your child practice the skills they're learning in therapy.

At the beginning of each session, the therapist will check in with your child to see how they're doing and see if there's anything they want to talk about. The therapist will then review the goals for treatment and plan the activities for that session.

Therapy activities will vary depending on your child's age, interests, and needs. Some common activities include:

- Discussing anxiety-provoking situations and brainstorming coping strategies.
- Role-playing to practice new skills.
- Exposure therapy to gradually face fears.
- Relaxation and breathing exercises.
- Journaling to track progress.
- Play therapy.
- Games and mental exercises.

- Other modalities like music therapy, physical therapy, or tension and trauma release exercises (TRE).

Your child's therapist will probably use a mix of these activities to create a treatment plan tailored to your child's individual needs.

At the end of each session, the therapist will ask your child how they feel and what they gained from the session. The therapist may also provide homework for your child to complete at home, review the goals for the next session, and give you some activities to practice in a real-life scenario. Although the therapist may not reveal everything discussed in each session, they should give you a general idea of what was covered and how your child is progressing.

After a few sessions, you and your child's therapist should see some progress. As your child feels better, the number of sessions will gradually decrease. The therapist may also recommend some resources or referrals for continued support after therapy.

Remember—progress can be slow, and there may be setbacks along the way. Just keep working with your child and their therapist, and don't give up hope. With time, patience, and hard work, your child will eventually overcome their anxiety. Be sure to express any concerns you have with the therapist so that they can be addressed.

HOW TO FIND A THERAPIST IN YOUR AREA

If you think exposure therapy may be right for your child, the first step is to find a therapist specializing in this type of treatment. You can ask your child's doctor for a referral or search for a therapist online. Two significant sources to help you find a therapist in your area are: https://www.findapsychologist.org/ and https://locator.apa.org/.

You can also check in with your state's psychological association or your insurance company to get a list of providers in your area. Ask for recommendations if you know anybody who has been to therapy or has a child in therapy. Once you have a list of potential therapists, you can narrow it down by reading their bios and looking at their websites. Choose a therapist who has experience treating children and specializes in exposure therapy. You should also make sure they're familiar with the specific type of exposure therapy you're interested in. To help you better understand what to look for in a therapist and their plan, the following chapter focuses on what to expect in each session.

7

SESSION BY SESSION

K nowing what to expect can hugely reduce any therapy-related anxiety for both the parent and child. So, here's an idea of what you might expect in each exposure therapy session. Please note that therapists will have their own preferred plans and schedules, so you will always need to discuss this in advance.

PHOBIAS OF LARGE ANIMALS AND DOGS

The first step is for the therapist and child to work together to create a fear ladder. This will involve listing all the activities related to the child's fear, starting with the least scary challenge to tackle. For instance, if a child fears dogs, the therapist may start by having the child look at pictures of dogs before gradually progressing to being in the same room as a real dog. Once the fear ladder is created, the therapist will work with the child to tackle their fears, one step at a time.

In order to be successful, the therapist may teach the child more about animals and how they interact with humans. Once the child understands dogs are not dangerous, they may feel more comfortable around them. The therapist will also help the child identify their triggers and what makes them anxious. This may involve discussing previous negative experiences or identifying core beliefs about animals.

For instance, the child may believe that all dogs are dangerous and will attack them. Once the child is more aware of their triggers and beliefs, they can challenge them. However, during this process, they might limit the interactions with triggers so as not to get overwhelmed.

The therapist will also work on teaching the child self-soothing techniques. This is important as it will help the child remain calm in the face of their fear. The therapist may teach the child deep breathing exercises or progressive muscle relaxation.

Keep in mind that each therapist has their own unique plan with specific steps that may vary from the ones listed above, and the number of sessions will also depend on the severity of the child's fear. For instance, a child with a mild fear of dogs may only need 6–8 sessions, whereas a child with a more severe fear may need up to 12–15 sessions. However, most therapists will generally use a combination of therapy, CBT skills, exposure therapy, virtual reality therapy, animal-assisted therapy, or medication to help the child.

PHOBIAS OF THE DARK

Similar to working with a phobia of animals, the therapist and child would create a fear ladder revolving around their fear of the dark so they can determine where to begin. Then the therapist might have your child sit in a dimly lit room for a short period and then gradually progress to sitting in a completely dark room.

As with other types of phobias, the therapist will help the child understand their triggers and what makes them anxious. Then the child will learn self-soothing techniques and exposure therapy. The therapist may use virtual reality therapy to help the child face their fear in a controlled environment. Other techniques the therapist may use are CBT techniques, hypnotherapy, psychotherapy, and mindful techniques.

FEARS OF DOING POORLY IN SCHOOL

The first step is to list all the activities related to the child's fear of doing poorly in school. For instance, they might be worried about a test or presentation. The therapist may use a questionnaire or art therapy to gauge your child's fear. Then the child can focus on tackling each of these fears, like taking steps up a ladder. The child may start by looking at pictures of people taking tests or giving presentations. They might have homework like joining a school play and socializing or going to a school dance to gain more confidence. Then the child identifies what triggers their fears.

For instance, the child may believe they are not smart enough to do well in school. Becoming aware of the negative beliefs is crucial. Then the child will learn coping mechanisms they can employ when they feel stressed and anxious. Aside from exposure therapy, the therapist may also use CBT techniques, hypnotherapy, and psychotherapy.

PHOBIAS OF NATURAL DISASTERS

Like with the other examples, the child creates a fear ladder by evaluating their anxieties. For example, the child may be afraid of thunderstorms, tornadoes, or floods. Then they'll implement self-soothing techniques and exposure therapy to accept their fears in a fun yet safe environment. Virtual reality exposure might be used as well. The therapist may start by showing movies or pictures of natural disasters. If the child is afraid of the dark, they might use virtual reality to shift from a dimly lit room to a dark room as the sessions progress.

The therapist may also discuss previous negative experiences or identify core beliefs about natural disasters. For instance, the child may be afraid because they think they are not safe during a natural disaster. Once your child understands their triggers and what causes them, they can challenge and reframe their beliefs. The therapist may use a combination of CBT techniques, hypnotherapy, psychotherapy, or virtual therapy.

OCD OF REPETITIVE BEHAVIORS AND UNWANTED THOUGHTS

To overcome OCD, the therapist might use therapy techniques like CBT, and exposure and response prevention (ERP), which is a specific type of CBT. According to the International OCD Foundation, "ERP is the most effective evidence-based treatment for OCD."

The therapist will create a detailed assessment to determine what the child's fears are and how severely they manifest. For example, the child may experience unwanted thoughts like "What if I get sick?" or "What if I hurt someone?" The therapist will assist the child in understanding their thoughts and help them challenge their beliefs.

The therapist will also help them identify what causes their repetitive behaviors. For example, the child may feel the need to sniff their fingers. The therapist will help them understand why they are doing this behavior and help them challenge their beliefs.

The therapist may combine techniques from other therapy practices if they feel it will help them ease more anxiety symptoms. They'll likely include the family and teach you how to support the child outside of therapy. They'll also decide if your child needs medication, therapy, or a combination of both.

OCD OF GERMS AND CONTAMINATION

To create the best treatment plan for OCD, the child would have to create a hierarchy that explains all their fears. For example, the child might be afraid of getting sick or touching contaminated surfaces. Then, the therapist will use soothing techniques, exposure therapy, and CBT techniques to assist the child in facing their fear in a controlled environment.

The therapist may have the child learn more about germs or watch videos about contamination. Once they understand how their triggers and thought processes affect them, they can challenge them. This is another instance where virtual reality therapy may help your child face their fears.

ANXIETY OF SOCIAL SITUATIONS

The therapist will complete an assessment identifying the child's triggers and what makes them nervous. For example, the child may be afraid of speaking in front of people or going to parties. The therapist will take each fear and ask what thoughts are associated with them so they can reframe their beliefs.

The therapist will also help them identify and practice coping mechanisms. For example, the child may need to practice deep breathing or relax their muscles when they feel anxious. Then they will work together to combine these techniques as they challenge their beliefs about their fears.

Exposure therapy will probably be the primary focus to prompt the child to challenge their fears in a safe and healthy manner. For instance, your child may watch videos or walk past a busy cafe. Then work their way up to having the child role-play various social situations with the therapist or in front of a mirror.

SESSIONS 1–10

Session 1

In general, most of these programs will follow a similar structure. Session 1 would be an overview of what the program will entail and an explanation of why this type of therapy is necessary. Then, the therapist will interview the child to understand their specific anxiety and what situations trigger it.

The therapist will also interview the family to gain a better understanding of the home environment and how the family can support the child. Your child may learn a coping mechanism or two, like a breathing exercise so that they can manage their anxiety on their own. Usually, homework would be assigned as well. All this information will create a more detailed action plan for your child to implement and conquer their anxieties.

Session 2

At the start of the second session, the therapist would review the homework from the previous session and help the child understand any concepts they may have struggled with. Then, your child would describe in detail their biggest fear and what situations trigger it. The therapist would help them understand how their thoughts are affecting their behavior. They'll speak about how your child reacts to traumatic or stressful situations.

After that, the therapist would help them challenge their thoughts and help them reframe their thinking. This is usually when exposure therapy would begin. The therapist would start with an easy exposure and work their way up to harder ones. For example, if the child is afraid of large animals, the therapist would start by having the child look at stills of large animals that trigger them. Then, they would work their way up to being in the same room as a larger animal. They might use techniques like in vivo desensitization, which is when the child is exposed to the real-life trigger, or imaginal desensitization, which is when the child challenges their fears in their mind. The therapist would help the child through the exposure and provide coping mechanisms as needed. Homework would likely be assigned for the child to practice in vivo techniques at home.

Session 3

In this session, the therapist will review the homework once again. If they don't review the homework and how the child did, then they might stop doing it. Therefore, keep an open conversation about the homework and their experiences completing the challenges. Thereafter, the therapist may prompt your child to use imaginal exposure therapy. The therapist would help the child imagine a situation that makes them anxious for 30–45 minutes and then provide coping mechanisms as needed. They will also likely have homework, like listening to the imaginal exposure recording, to practice at home that they will review in the next session.

Session 4

This session follows a similar format to Session 3. The therapist would review the homework and walk through any challenges they may have faced. Then, your child would describe the challenges they face. And then, together, they would work to comprehend their thoughts and the effect of their thoughts on their behavior.

After that, the therapist would reframe their thoughts and triggered emotions by using imaginal exposure therapy that works best for your child. As your child progresses, the therapist would expose them to harder and harder situations until they can cope with their anxiety on their own. Your child will also have to complete in vivo-focused homework to revisit the following session.

Session 5

This session will start like the other ones, with a review of the homework and talking about the challenges they faced. After reviewing the homework, they will practice exposure therapy techniques. The therapist will increase the duration and intensity of the exposure until your child is no longer anxious about the trigger. The therapist may also introduce new triggers to work on. The homework for this session will probably revisit previous triggers in vivo so they can continue to practice their exposure therapy and coping mechanisms.

Session 6

This session starts with reviewing the homework and how the child is feeling about their progress. The therapist will probably introduce new triggers to work on and help the child challenge their thoughts and reframe their thinking. This session might also include a review of all the exposure therapy techniques and coping mechanisms that have been learned. The therapist would help the child identify which ones work best for them and how to use them. The homework for this session will be to practice the exposure therapy techniques and coping mechanisms already learned.

Session 7

This session will review the homework and all the progress that has been made. The therapist and the child will work together to determine where there's room for improvement.

The therapist would help the child create a plan to continue practicing what they have learned and how to use the exposure therapy techniques and coping mechanisms in their daily life.

The therapist might also talk about any future triggers that may surface and how to deal with them. The homework for this session is to continue practicing the exposure therapy techniques and coping mechanisms. As they near the end of the sessions, the therapist will reassess their triggers. If their triggers are decreasing, imaginal exposure may be decreased, but in vivo exposure may continue.

Session 8

After a review of the homework, the therapist and the child will talk about how they have been doing and if they have been able to use what they've learned in their daily life. Depending on the assessment of their fears, the therapist may start to taper off of imaginal exposure and move toward in vivo exposure only. The therapist will work with the child to identify any areas that still need improvement and continue working on what they have learned. For homework, your child may likely continue practicing the techniques they've learned.

Session 9

This session begins by reviewing the previous assignment and determining how the child is feeling about their time in therapy. Since the end of the program is coming close, they might together note any room for improvement and create an action plan to continue using the techniques they have learned. The therapist discusses future challenges that may arise and how the child can use the techniques they've learned. The homework will focus on practicing old techniques and preparing for the last session.

Session 10

This is the last session! The therapist will review all the progress that has been made and help the child identify any areas that still need improvement. They will go over their plan to see what they remember and review how to use the new techniques in their daily life. They will revisit the traumatic experience one more time, but likely for twenty minutes at the most, and discuss the changes the child has experienced from the first session.

Together, they'll review the plan the child completed and the progress they've made. The last part of the session will include an in-depth review of how to apply everything they've learned in the future in the event of a trigger. The homework for this session is to continue applying their newfound skills throughout their lives.

The number of sessions needed will vary from child to child. Some may need more, and some may need less. It all depends on the severity of their anxiety and how well they respond to therapy.

Child psychology concentrates on the mental and emotional development of children. It can treat children who have anxiety disorders. Child psychology can help children to understand their thoughts and feelings and how to cope with them. With the help of a child psychologist, children can learn how to deal with their anxiety and live a normal life. In most cases, exposure therapy can be more helpful than CBT for children with anxiety disorders. However, your child might benefit from a combination of therapeutic techniques. It all depends on what works best for your child.

Anxiety is a normal and common emotion that everyone experiences at different times in their life. However, for some people, anxiety can be more intense and persistent, which can interfere with their daily life. If your child is struggling with anxiety, there are things you can do to help them. By teaching them about anxiety and how to manage it, they can feel more in control of themselves and their fears.

Keep in mind that these techniques also include homework. While your child will likely be able to complete some of these exercises on their own, they also need positive rein-forcement and maybe a little extra help. Fortunately, there are a few extra aspects you can consider to manage anxiety.

8

ALTERNATIVE AND HOLISTIC OPTIONS

Just because you fail once, doesn't mean you're failing at everything. Keep trying, hold on, and always trust yourself, because if you don't then who will?

— MARILYN MONROE

A nxiety can make people feel like they don't have power over themselves, especially when they're young and still struggling to find their footing in the world. When this happens, some people may turn to drugs or alcohol to try to cope. However, this is not a healthy solution and can actually make anxiety worse. If jumping right into therapy techniques or medication doesn't seem the right fit for you or your child, other options are still available.

The holistic approach treats the whole child, as we know brain and body are linked. This method uses a combination of therapies that address the physical, emotional, and mental aspects of anxiety. Holistic therapies can include things like yoga, meditation, aromatherapy, and massage. These therapies promote relaxation and serenity, which can reduce anxiety. However, the overall goal is to make sure the child receives genuine support and their needs are being met so they can manage their anxiety in a healthy way.

INTENSIVE EXPOSURE THERAPY

Typically, therapy for anxiety can last anywhere from several weeks to several months. However, some children may need a more intensive treatment approach. For children with severe anxiety or those who have not responded well to other forms of treatment, intensive exposure therapy might be the right approach.

Intensive exposure therapy is a treatment that involves spending many hours per day and five to seven days per week in therapy. This type of treatment is typically provided in an outpatient setting, meaning your child doesn't have to stay there throughout the whole treatment. However, some children may need to stay in a residential treatment center or hospital during therapy.

Intensive exposure therapy is a highly structured treatment that involves gradually facing the things your child is afraid of. The therapist will work with your child to create a hierarchy of feared situations, starting with the least triggering situation and working up to the most. Your child will then systematically face each fear, starting with the least anxiety-provoking situation.

As your child faces their fears, they will probably experience some discomfort and anxiety. The therapist will help your child cope with these feelings and work through the tough situations. With time, your child will learn that they can handle their anxiety and that their fears are manageable. This will help reduce the overall anxiety level and improve your child's quality of life.

The treatment plan for these sessions depends on the therapist and the needs of the child. You can, however, request the plans in advance. Common activities during intensive exposure therapy include:

- Discussing anxiety-provoking situations and brainstorming coping strategies.
- Role-playing of feared situations.
- Gradually exposing your child to real-life anxiety-provoking situations.
- Teaching breathing exercises and relaxation techniques.
- Practicing self-care and healthy coping strategies.

Intensive exposure therapy can be intense for both the child and the family. Make sure that you and your child(ren) are prepared for this type of treatment before you start. Be sure to ask the therapist questions you have and clarify anything you don't understand. Having a reliable support system in place is also crucial to help you and your child through this tough time.

THE BASICS

Our bodies affect our brains and vice versa. When our needs are met and we feel good physically, it's easier to manage our emotions and thoughts. For example, if we're hungry, tired, or in pain, it's harder to focus, and we're more likely to feel anxious or stressed. Therefore, taking care of our physical needs is crucial in managing anxiety.

Some basic things that can help include:

Quality Sleep

Children need more sleep than adults, typically around 10 hours a day. A lack of sleep can make anxiety worse. There are four stages of sleep. Two are light sleep stages, where it's easier for the person to be woken. Then there's deep sleep, which is when the body repairs and regenerates.

Deep sleep is the most refreshing sleep; however, night terrors, bedwetting, and sleepwalking are common in this stage. The last stage is rapid eye movement (REM) sleep, which is when we dream. Receiving a healthy mix of all four stages is critical in order to feel rested. Each stage has important qualities, and without enough of it, we can feel fatigued and anxious. Common signs that your child might need more sleep are:

- Crankiness, irritability, or whininess.
- Poor concentration.
- Falling asleep during the day.
- Struggling with schoolwork.
- Hyperactivity.
- Behavioral problems.

Exercise

Exercise releases endorphins, which have mood-boosting properties. Endorphins can also reduce stress and improve sleep. Ideally, children ages 6 to 17 need at least 60 minutes of exercise a day. Toddlers should have about three hours of active play throughout the day, whether it's active free play or an activity led by an adult. This doesn't mean your child needs to be enrolled in after-school sports, but they should move their bodies every day.

There are three elements of exercise:

Endurance: This is when the heart and lungs have to work harder, such as running, biking, or swimming. Popular endurance examples for children are playing tag, running around the playground, or riding a bike. As they get older, they can engage in activities like ice skating, bicycling, soccer, tennis, or swimming.

Strengthening: This includes activities that use muscles to work against gravity, such as climbing or gymnastics. For adults, this may include lifting weights, but for children, they can do simple body-weight exercises like crunches, pull-ups, push-ups, or handstands. Children can use playground equipment, such as the monkey bars, or use common household items to create an obstacle course.

Flexibility: This involves stretching and moving the joints through their full range of motion, such as in yoga or tai chi, martial arts, stretching, practicing a split, dancing, or practicing a cartwheel.

A Healthy Diet

Similar to adults, a child's diet can alter their emotions, thought processes, and energy levels. Our gut and brains are connected via the vagus nerve, and what we eat can either help or hurt our gut bacteria. If the gut is receiving poor nutrition, then that travels to the brain and can impact how we're feeling. On the other hand, how our brain feels can also affect our digestion and what we're craving. It's a two-way street!

Some tips for a healthy diet include:

- Eating regular meals and snacks.

- Avoiding processed foods, sugary drinks, and excessive amounts of caffeine.
- Eating plenty of fruits, vegetables, whole grains, and lean protein.

Some kid-friendly foods that can ease anxiety are:

- Yogurt: provides probiotics, which are good bacteria for gut health.
- Oranges and vitamin C: can help reduce stress.
- Omega-3 fatty acids: found in fish, can improve mood and cognitive function.
- Chamomile tea: can be a relaxing drink, especially before bed. Add stevia or honey if your child prefers a sweeter drink.
- Almonds: an excellent source of magnesium, which can relax muscles.
- Turkey or tryptophan: an amino acid that helps the body produce serotonin, which can improve mood.
- Water: helps the body function properly and can also help to reduce fatigue.
- Eggs: a superb source of protein and B vitamins, which can help with energy levels.

Eliminate Inflammation-Inducing Foods

Inflammation can be a cause of anxiety and can also worsen symptoms. Foods that can contribute to inflammation are:

- Processed foods
- Sugar
- Trans fats
- Processed meats
- Refined carbs
- Foods that contain gluten
- Dairy products

Some foods that can help to reduce inflammation are:

- Green leafy vegetables
- Nuts and seeds
- Oily fish
- Olive oil
- Fruit and vegetables
- Garlic
- Ginger

Proper Hydration

Water is essential for our bodies to function properly. It helps to carry nutrients to our cells, flush out toxins, and regulate body temperature. When we're dehydrated, our bodies can't function properly, and that can lead to fatigue, headaches, and even anxiety. Drink plenty of water throughout the day, especially when you're feeling stressed or anxious.

Supplements

If a child is not getting enough of certain nutrients from their diet, a doctor may recommend supplements. Some common supplements for anxiety are:

- Omega-3 fatty acids

Can improve mood and cognitive function. Look for supplements that also include vitamin D, which helps the body absorb omega-3s.

- Magnesium

Can relax muscles and reduce anxiety. Magnesium can be found in rice, oats, and wheats, but once they're processed, they lose a lot of the magnesium content. Sunflower seeds, pumpkin seeds, and dark chocolate are also unimpeachable sources of magnesium.

- Vitamin B complex

Helps the body produce serotonin, which can enhance positive emotions. Excellent sources of vitamin B include poultry, eggs, fish, and dark leafy greens.

- Lavender or chamomile

Can be used as a tea or in aromatherapy. Chamomile tea is especially helpful for children who have trouble sleeping.

- Passionflower

Can improve anxiety or GI problems. Passionflower is sometimes combined with other herbs, such as chamomile or lemon balm, for additional benefits.

While supplements can be helpful, speak with a doctor before giving them to a child. Supplements can interact with medications, and some may not be appropriate for children.

ALTERNATIVE THERAPIES

In addition to diet and supplements, several alternative therapies can help to reduce anxiety. Some common ones are:

Tension and Trauma Releasing Exercises

TRE is a type of exercise that helps to acknowledge and release the strains that can build up in the body from stress. It can be done by anyone but talk with a doctor or certified TRE provider first. TRE exercises can include:

- Stretching
- Breathing exercises
- Shaking or trembling

- Massage
- Yoga

TRE has been helpful for adults with PTSD and may also be beneficial for children who have experienced trauma.

Music and Gong Therapy

Music therapy can help to reduce anxiety by providing a soothing activity. It can also prompt children to express their emotions creatively. Gong therapy is a type of music therapy that uses gongs to create relaxing sounds that can help reduce stress. Music therapy makes a difference because it stimulates the senses, motivates children, encourages socialization and self-expression, and can provide a sense of control, which can help to improve mood.

Music therapy can help many people who struggle in various ways. According to Harmony Music Therapy, after engaging in music therapy, a 6-year-old boy with Autism began to speak and use phrases to communicate instead of throwing tantrums. He also would say "hello" to his grandmother—something he never did in his six years. Additionally, after just a few sessions, he was more interactive and communicative with his classmates.

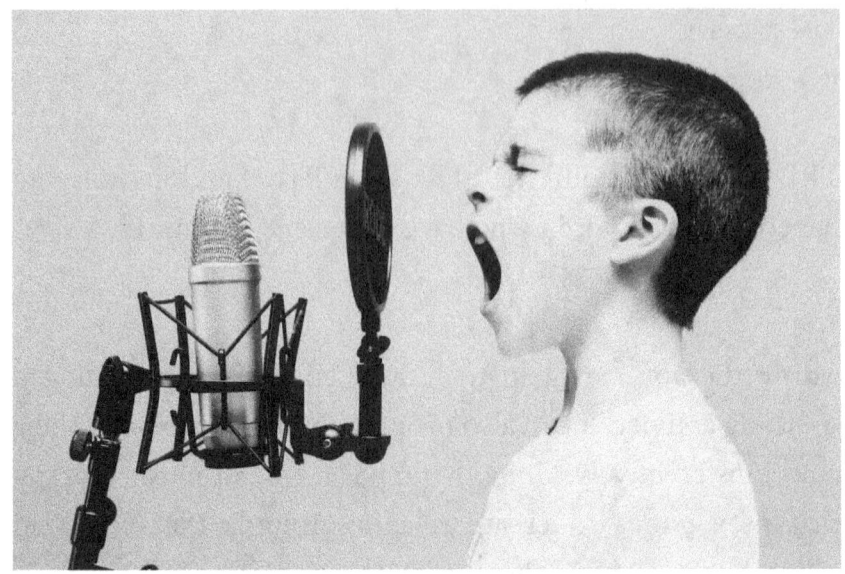

Sand Tray Therapy

Sand tray therapy is a combination of art and play therapy that uses sand and miniature figures to help children express themselves. Children can use the box to create a pretend world using the items. They can explore their emotions, work through trauma, and resolve conflict. Sand tray therapy can be helpful for children who have a difficult time communicating their feelings. Sand tray play can reduce anxiety by providing a safe and calming space for children to express themselves.

Movement or Dance Therapy

Movement therapy can improve emotions and reduce nervousness. It can also help to improve coordination, balance, and strength. Dance therapy is a type of movement therapy that uses dance to improve mental and physical health. Dance therapy can help children who have trouble expressing their emotions because it can help them understand and respect their limitations. Other benefits include:

- Express themselves and communicate with others better.
- Reduce body tension or chronic pain.
- Increase body awareness, creativity, and a positive body image.
- Establish a new relationship with their bodies.

OTHER FORMS OF THERAPY

In some cases, exposure therapy may not be the best treatment approach. This is typically the case for children with very severe anxiety or those who have difficulty tolerating the discomfort of exposure therapy. In these cases, the therapist may recommend another form of therapy, such as:

Cognitive-behavioral therapy: This type of therapy focuses on altering the negative and self-destroying thoughts or beliefs that contribute to anxiety.

Family therapy: This type of therapy can improve the way you communicate and problem-solve as a family. It can also provide support for the child and family members.

Play therapy: This type of therapy uses play to help the child express their thoughts and feelings. It can also teach coping skills.

Generalized anxiety disorder therapy: This type of therapy focuses on teaching the child how to manage anxiety in all areas of life using evidence-based treatments. This may include CBT skills, medication, or a combination of both.

OCD therapy: A therapist works with the child to teach them how to manage anxiety using evidence-based treatments, like CBT skills and exposure therapy.

Exposure therapy: This approach is the focus of this book and aims to help a child face their fears in a safe and gradual way. The plan includes creating exposure hierarchies and gradually working up to the most anxiety-provoking situations. The therapist and the child agree on a goal and create a fear ladder based on anxieties, progress, and mastery.

During this time, your child will need support as the exposure tactics often vary and escalate as the child becomes more confident. However, before they can tackle their fear ladders, your child needs to learn self-soothing techniques so they can manage anxiety and remain calm in the face of fear. This technique will not only help them while they are challenging their fears but in all areas of their life where they experience anxiety.

Zen Meditation and Practices

Zen meditation is a type of mindfulness meditation that can help to improve focus and concentration. It can also help to reduce anxiety by teaching people how to be present in the moment and focus on their breath. Zen meditation can be helpful for children who struggle to sit still or have a lot of racing thoughts. Zen practices can include yoga, tai chi, and qigong. You can fill a diffuser with your child's favorite scent to help them relax during meditation.

Psychodrama

Psychodrama is a type of therapy that uses role-playing and storytelling to help children express themselves. In this process, children may act out scenes from their lives or from stories. This can help them understand and process their emotions. Psychodrama can be beneficial for children who have trouble communicating their emotions. Psychodrama can help children to:

- Express themselves.
- Resolve conflict.
- Work through trauma.
- Improve communication and social skills.
- Build self-esteem.

Puppetry

Puppetry is a type of therapy that uses puppets to help children express themselves. Children can use a variety of puppets, including hand puppets, marionettes, and shadow puppets, to create a scene or story. Puppetry can prompt children who struggle to share and convey their feelings or thoughts in a different way. It can also help children work through trauma, resolve conflict, and build self-esteem.

Reiki

Reiki is a type of energy therapy that can help to reduce stress and promote relaxation. It is safe and noninvasive, which is a great option for children who are weary of therapy. This practice can be helpful for children who have difficulty sleeping or are experiencing anxiety. Reiki can also help to improve attention spans and concentration efforts. By learning to practice reiki early in life, children can develop positive skills that will assist them with coping throughout their lives. Reiki can help to:

- Reduce stress and anxiety.
- Promote relaxation.
- Improve sleep.
- Reduce pain.
- Improve mood.
- Promote balance.
- Boosts self-awareness.

Naturopathy

Naturopathy is a type of alternative medicine that uses natural treatments to promote healing. This can include a variety of modalities, such as nutrition, herbal medicine, and acupuncture. Naturopathy can be helpful for children who are looking for a more holistic approach to their health. It can also be helpful for children who have chronic health conditions or who are dealing with anxiety or stress. Naturopathy can help to:

- Improve overall health.
- Boost immunity.
- Reduce stress and anxiety.
- Promote relaxation.
- Treat chronic conditions.

Acupuncture

Acupuncture is an alternative medicine that involves the insertion of thin needles into the body. Acupuncture can treat a variety of conditions, such as pain, anxiety, and stress. Acupuncture can be a helpful treatment for children who are unwilling to take medication. It is safe and effective and has few side effects. Acupuncture can help to:

- Reduce pain.
- Relieve stress and anxiety.
- Improve mood.
- Promote relaxation.
- Boost immunity.

However, acupuncture should only be used for children over eight years old. For children under eight, they can do Shonishin, which is a type of acupuncture that uses gentle touch instead of needles. They can also choose to do acupressure or Tuina massage, which are both gentle versions of acupuncture performed by trained professionals.

Ayurveda

Ayurveda is a type of alternative medicine conducted by a practitioner that uses a variety of modalities to promote healing. This can include nutrition, herbal medicine, and massage. Ayurveda can be helpful for those looking for a more holistic approach. This practice can help relieve the common cold, earaches, seasonal allergies, stomachaches, and sleep.

Biofeedback

Biofeedback is a type of therapy that uses sensors to measure the body's response to stress. A biofeedback therapist, who is usually a medical provider, conducts this process and uses information to help the child learn to control their body's response to stress. Biofeedback can treat a variety of conditions, such as chronic pain and nervousness, and reduce anxiety attacks. It is a safe and effective approach.

Hypnotherapy

Hypnotherapy is a type of therapy that uses relaxation and visualization techniques to help the child reach a state of deep relaxation. This technique is accomplished by a licensed therapist or a trained professional. In this state, the child is more open to suggestions and can be helped to overcome a variety of issues, such as fear, anxiety, and stress. Hypnotherapy is safe and prompts reliable results.

Art Therapy

Art therapy is a type of therapy that uses art to help the child express their emotions. This can be a helpful way for children to process their feelings and to learn new coping skills. They may practice watercolor, sculpting, painting, coloring, or drawing. Art therapy can assist with the treatment of a variety of conditions, such as anxiety, stress, and trauma.

Yoga

Yoga is a type of exercise that uses physical postures, breathing techniques, and meditation to promote relaxation and well-being. This holistic approach also offers dual benefits by prompting regular exercise. Yoga can help to:

- Relieve stress and anxiety.
- Improve mood.
- Promote relaxation.
- Boost immunity.

Mindfulness Exercises

Mindfulness exercises are a type of therapy that uses breathing and meditation techniques to help the child focus on the present moment. The therapist will teach these to your child, so they can implement them when feeling anxious. Some examples are:

- Focusing on the breath.
- Listening to the sounds around you.
- Noticing the sensations in your body.
- Observing your thoughts and emotions.

Mindfulness exercises like breathing techniques or meditation can benefit children who are dealing with anxiety or stress. Mindfulness exercises can help to:

- Relieve stress and anxiety.
- Improve mood.
- Promote relaxation.
- Boost immunity.

Ultimately, it's about providing as many tools as possible so our children can thrive. From coping mechanisms to handling their fears to praises so they can feel more encouraged—empowering your child will help build confidence and courage.

9

BUILD CONFIDENCE

Optimism is the faith that leads to achievement. Nothing can be done without hope and confidence.

— HELEN KELLER

It is essential to be optimistic and have hope when taking on parenting. Optimism is defined as having a positive outlook toward life and expecting the best to happen. It is a self-fulfilling prophecy where our positive thoughts result in positive actions and ultimately produce positive outcomes.

Some benefits of being an optimistic parent include:

- You will be more likely to see the best in your child

When you are optimistic, you are more likely to focus on your child's strengths and positive qualities. This will help you have a better relationship with your child as you will see their potential and encourage them to reach their goals.

- You will be more likely to take on challenges

Optimistic parents are more likely to take on parenting challenges as they believe they can overcome them. This can cause a more positive parenting experience, as you will feel more capable and confident in your abilities.

- You will be more likely to persevere

Optimistic parents are more likely to persevere through difficult times as they have faith that the situation will eventually improve. This can lead to a more positive outcome, as you will more likely stick with your parenting goals even when times are tough.

TIPS FOR INCREASING OPTIMISM

Work on Your Child's Self-Esteem

One way to increase optimism in your parenting is to work on your child's self-esteem. This can be done by complimenting your child regularly, encouraging them to try new things, and helping them to set realistic goals.

Help Your Child Master New Skills and Tasks

At every age, there are new activities for kids to learn or challenges to overcome. When they feel good about their abilities, it boosts self-esteem and promotes optimism. When you're teaching your child to do something new, give clear directions, and praise their efforts along the way. It may be helpful to show them how to do it, so they have an example to follow. You can also make it into a game or use positive reinforcement to help them learn.

Praise Your Child's Efforts and Successes

You can help increase your child's self-esteem by praising their efforts and successes, no matter how small. Be honest and keep your tone positive. For example, you can say, "Great job trying new things!" or "I'm proud of how hard you're working!" This will help boost their confidence in themselves and their abilities.

Be a Good Role Model

You can increase optimism in your parenting by being an exemplary role model. This means you should try to be positive and optimistic about yourself. You can do this by talking about the good things in your life, staying positive when things go wrong, and setting a good example for your child to follow.

Some ways to be an excellent role model include:

• Talk about the good things in your life

When you talk about the good things in your life, you are teaching your child to focus on the positive. This will help them see the glass as half full rather than half empty.

• Stay positive when things go wrong

When a situation veers off course, stay positive. This will teach your child that it's okay to feel sad or angry but not to let these emotions take over.

• Set a good example

You can set a good example for your child by being a positive and optimistic person yourself. This will teach them that it's possible to be happy and successful even when things are tough.

Ban Harsh Criticism

Harsh criticism can be detrimental to a child's self-esteem and confidence, which can lead to pessimism. Avoid criticizing your child harshly, as this can make them feel like they don't have the knowledge or the abilities to complete the task.

Instead of criticizing, try to focus on the positive. For example, if your child makes a mistake, you can say, "That's okay, everyone makes mistakes. What's important is that you learn from it and try not to make the same mistake again." This will help your child to feel good about themselves and to see mistakes as a learning opportunity.

Encourage an Attitude of Gratitude

An attitude of gratitude can help to increase optimism in both you and your child. This means you should focus on the benefits in life you are thankful for rather than on the things that are going wrong.

Some ways to encourage an attitude of gratitude include:

- Expressing gratitude

One way to encourage gratitude is to express it yourself. You can do this by thanking your child for their help, complimenting them on their achievements, or simply telling them how much you appreciate them.

- Keeping a gratitude journal

You can encourage your child to keep a gratitude journal, where they write down positive aspects in their lives for which they are thankful. This can be things like a good day at school, a fun weekend, or anything that has made them happy.

- Focusing on the positive

Another way to encourage gratitude is to focus on the positive things in your child's life. This will help them see the good even when things are tough.

Focus on Strengths

When you praise your child's strengths, you are teaching them to focus on and strengthen their positive aspects. This will help to increase their optimism and self-esteem.

Some ways to focus on your child's strengths include:

- Complimenting their strengths

Compliment your child's strengths. This can be things like "You're so good at art!" or "I'm proud of how hard you worked on that project."

- Encouraging their strengths

Another way to concentrate on your child's positive attributes is to encourage them. This can be things like "I know you can do it!" or "I believe in you."

- Helping them to develop their strengths

You can also help your child to develop their strengths by providing opportunities for them to use their talents. For example, if they are good at art, you can sign them up for an art class. If they are good at sports, you can enroll them in a sport.

Prompt Kids to Help and Give to Others

Teaching your child to help and give to others is a great way to encourage optimism. Optimism keeps us positive and helps us see the world in a brighter light.

Some ways to encourage your child to help and give to others include:

- Help at home

One way to help and give to others is by helping at home. These can be activities like doing the dishes, taking out the trash, or vacuuming the floors.

- Help out at school

Another way to assist and provide for others is to help at school. This can be things like picking up trash in the hallway, helping a friend with their work, or participating in a school fundraiser.

- Help the community

You can also help and give to others by helping in the community. This can be things like volunteering at a local shelter, collecting food for a food drive, or participating in a community cleanup day.

The child should feel grateful for what they have rather than feeling entitled to things. This will help them be more appreciative of life and view aspects from a positive angle instead of a negative one.

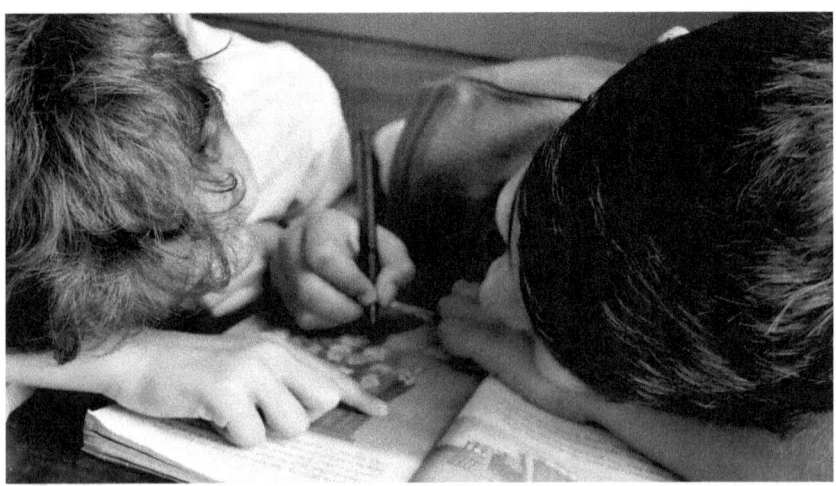

Hand Over the Power

One way to increase optimism in your child is to hand over the power. This means giving them choices and letting them make decisions. They'll feel more in control, which will ultimately lead to a more optimistic outlook. You can help them achieve a sense of responsibility by letting them choose which parts of family life they would like to contribute to. Let them manage and plan these tasks in their own time to avoid any pressure they may feel.

Some ways to hand over the power include:

- Asking them for their opinion

One way to hand over the power is to ask your child for their opinion. This can be things like "Which shirt do you want to wear today?" or "What do you want to eat for dinner?"

- Giving them choices

Another way to hand over the power is to give your child choices. These can be things like "Do you want to watch TV or read a book?" or "Do you want to go to the park or the zoo?"

- Allowing them to decide

You can also allow your child to make decisions. This can mean asking them, "What do you want to do this weekend?" or "Where do you want to go on vacation?"

Encourage Them to Be Resilient

Teaching your child to be resilient is another great way to encourage optimism because resilient people know how to reset themselves after a setback. They know to focus on the present moment and the current positives they have instead of ruminating over their failures.

There are many ways to encourage resilience in your child, but some of the most effective ways include:

- Helping them to problem-solve

One way to encourage resilience is to help your child to problem-solve. This means teaching them how to identify and solve problems on their own.

- Encouraging them to persevere

Another way to encourage resilience is to encourage your child to persevere. This means teaching them how to keep going, even when things are tough.

- Helping them to set goals

You can also help your child to set goals. This means teaching them how to set realistic goals and achieve them according to their plan.

- Showing them how to fix mistakes

Finally, you can show your child how to fix mistakes. This means teaching them that mistakes are okay and that they can learn from them. For example, if they make a mistake in their homework, you can help them fix it.

- Teaching them how to apologize and make amends

Another important lesson to teach your child is how to apologize and make amends. This means teaching them it's okay to make mistakes but that they need to be accountable for their actions. If they hurt someone, they should apologize.

- Teaching them to embrace mistakes as learning opportunities

Finally, you can teach your child to embrace mistakes as learning opportunities. This means teaching them that mistakes are a natural part of life and that they can learn from them. For example, if they make a mistake in school, you can help them learn from it.

- Promoting success

One of the best ways to encourage optimism is to promote success. Engaging in challenges or learning new things is beneficial for kids, but so is seeing themselves as successful. As a parent, you can help your child see themselves as successful by setting them up for success. For example, you can give them tasks that are age appropriate and within their abilities. You can also praise them when they do well and provide encouragement when they make mistakes. Prompt your child to engage in activities that make them feel confident enough to tackle more triggering challenges. You can encourage them to try extra activities or have them help others.

Optimism is a noble trait to have, and it's one you can encourage in your child. By teaching your child how to be resilient, setting them up for success, and promoting positive thinking, you can help them develop a more optimistic outlook on life. Be on the lookout for when things go right and celebrate the small wins.

10

CELEBRATE SUCCESSES

The more you praise and celebrate your life, the more there is in life to celebrate.

— OPRAH WINFREY

As a parent, it's important to celebrate your child's successes. This not only helps them to feel good about themselves but also encourages them to continue striving for success. Celebrating your child's success is a great way to show them that you are proud of them and that you support their efforts. This can nourish and encourage their growth and promote their progress. Praising everyday achievements and their accomplishments in therapy can be very beneficial for your child.

There are many ways to celebrate your child's successes. You can praise them verbally, hug them or give them a high five. You can also write them a note of encouragement, give them a special treat, or take them out for ice cream. Whatever you do, make sure your child knows you are proud of their accomplishments.

It's also important to encourage your child to celebrate their own successes. This means teaching them how to take pride in their accomplishments and to feel good about themselves. You can do this by helping them to set goals and then congratulating them when they reach their goals. You can also encourage them to talk about their successes with others and to share their accomplishments with you. Here are a few other things to keep in mind:

Never present empty praises: When you praise your child, make sure that it is genuine and honest. Avoid simply telling your child, "Good job," with no explanation. This can come across as insincere and can actually devalue their accomplishments. Explain to them why the achievement is commendable and how it benefits them.

Be aware of overpraising: It's also important to avoid overpraising your child. Overly praising can also make your child feel that your approval and love are conditional, depending on their performance and achievement, and can lead to a sense of entitlement. Only praise their accomplishments when they have truly earned them.

Praise their effort, not their ability: Focus on praising your child's effort rather than their ability. This will help them see that they can improve with hard work and dedication. It will also encourage them to keep trying, even when they make mistakes.

Praise appropriately: Make sure your praise is appropriate for your child's age and development. For example, avoid using phrases like "You're such a good girl" with a toddler. This can make them feel as though they have to be perfect in order to please you. With older children, you can be more specific in your praise. For example, you might say, "Great job on your math test!" or "You did a really marvelous job of cleaning up your room." Also, keep the praise proportional to the achievements. For example, if your child gets an A on their math test, you wouldn't want to say, "You're the best math student ever!" This would be over the top and could lead to unrealistic expectations.

Be specific in your praise: Another way to make sure your praise is effective is to be specific. This means avoiding general comments like "Good job." Instead, focus on the specifics of what your child did you are proud of. For example, you might say, "I'm so proud of you for working so hard on your English essay!" or "You did a great job of staying calm when your sister made you angry." This will help your child understand that what they did was successful and will encourage them to continue doing it.

Avoid using criticism: It's also important to avoid using criticism when you are praising your child. This means avoiding comments like "You're so lazy" or "You're such a klutz." These types of comments can actually undermine your child's confidence and make them less likely to succeed.

Consider random awards: A fun way to encourage your child and make them feel good about their accomplishments is to give them random awards. For example, you might give them a "Most-Improved Player" award if they have been working hard to improve their grades. Or you might give them a "Superstar" award for doing a great job at home. These types of awards will make your child feel appreciated and will encourage them to keep up the good work. Don't make the reward the same each time as it then becomes an expectation and loses its value as recognition for effort.

Make a big deal out of minor accomplishments: It's also important to make a big deal out of your child's minor accomplishments. They will feel positive about themselves and be encouraged to keep up the good work. For example, if your child cleans up their room without being asked, praise them for it. You might say, "Wow! You did a great job of cleaning up your room! I'm so proud of you!"

The bottom line is that praising your child's successes in a genuine, honest, and appropriate way will help them feel positive about what they're doing and continue striving for success.

HOW TO CELEBRATE THEIR SUCCESSES

When your child achieves something great, celebrate their success in a way that is appropriate for their age and development. Here are a few tips:

With younger children, try to keep the celebrations short and sweet. This means avoiding things like parades and parties. Instead, consider having a small celebration at home with cake or ice cream.

You can be a bit more creative in your celebrations with older children. For example, consider having a party or taking them out to dinner.

Whatever you do, focus on the positives, and avoid making comparisons with other children. Your child will feel more accomplished and prompted to continue striving for success.

Verbal Praise

When praising your child, words are powerful. In fact, research has shown that verbal praise can actually be more effective than material rewards.

The first step is to make sure your praise is genuine and honest. This means avoiding comments like "You're the best child ever!" This would be over the top, and your child would likely see right through it. Instead, try focusing on specific things your child has done well.

You might say, "I'm so proud of you for studying for that math test!" or "You did a great job of expressing your feelings." Make sure the link between the behavior and the praise is clear to your child.

Rewards

While verbal praise is important, it's also important to consider using rewards to encourage your child.

Here are a few tips for using rewards:

- Make sure the rewards are appropriate

Make sure that the rewards you give are appropriate for your child's age and development. For example, a young child might be motivated by a small toy or a special treat, while an older child might be motivated by a privilege, such as staying up an extra half hour.

- Don't overdo it

It's also important to avoid giving too many rewards, as this can create a sense of entitlement. Instead, focus on giving rewards for enormous accomplishments or for sustained effort over time.

- Make sure the rewards are consistent

Finally, ensure the rewards you give are consistent. This means avoiding things like randomly giving a toy as a reward and then presenting them with money. Make it clear what they're working toward and why.

Treats

As a reward, you can present your child with a treat, such as a food or drink. For example, you might say, "Good job on that test! Here's a special treat for you." Just be sure to avoid giving too many treats, as this can lead to unhealthy habits.

Privileges

You can also use privileges as rewards. For example, you might say, "Good job of cleaning your room! You can stay up an extra half hour tonight." Just make sure that the privilege is appropriate for your child.

Quality Time

Another great way to reward your child is by spending quality time with them. This can be anything from reading a book together to going for a walk. Just focus on them and give them your undivided attention.

Let Them Choose

A final tip is to let your child choose their own rewards. They will feel more in control of the situation and motivated to achieve their goals. For example, you might say, "Good job with your chores! What would you like to do as a reward?" This will give them a sense of ownership and accountability for their own achievements. If you're worried about what they might choose, consider listing various age-appropriate options for them to choose from.

Plan a Party or a Special Dinner

Depending on the accomplishment, plan a party or special dinner to celebrate your child's success. This is a great way to show them how proud you are of their achievements. Just be sure to clarify that the party is a reward for their accomplishments.

Time Off from Chores

You might also want to give your child a break from their regular chores as a reward. This will give them some extra free time to enjoy themselves. Just be sure to clarify that the break is a reward for their accomplishments. For instance, if they did well on their history test, you might say, "Good job! You don't have to wash the dishes tonight."

Create a Collage or an Award for Their Accomplishments

You can also create a collage or award to commemorate your child's accomplishments to convey how proud you are of what they've accomplished. For example, you might say, "Good job on your math test! Here's a special award for you." Or you can take all their hard work and create a collage to showcase in the home. This can highlight their successes for everyone to see.

Use Star Charts

Star charts are a great way to visually track your child's progress and achievements. This can help them see how well they're doing and provide motivation to keep up the good work. For example, you might say, "Every time you do your homework without complaining, you get a star. Once you get ten stars, you can choose a reward." This will help them see the direct connection between their actions and the rewards they receive.

Spread the News to Family and Friends

You can also spread the news of your child's accomplishments to their family and friends. For instance, you can tell your child, "Good job on your math test! I'm going to call grandma and tell her all about it." This will help your child to feel appreciated and supported in their efforts.

These are just a few ideas for how you can reward your child for their accomplishments. Be sure to clarify that the reward is for their accomplishments. This will help them make the connection between their actions and the reward, so they feel motivated and supported in their efforts.

CONCLUSION

Exposure therapy is a type of treatment that prompts children to challenge and conquer their fears and anxieties. After completing exposure therapy, about 60% to 90% of people experience little to no symptoms of their anxiety disorder. However, the concerns about exposure therapy cause many parents to avoid it.

In order to help your child succeed in exposure therapy, you need to be informed and get the help of a professional. With the proper techniques and unconditional support, your child can manage their anxiety and lead a more exciting and healthy life. Here's a brief reminder of what you've learned:

- Exposure therapy focuses on helping people confront their fears in a controlled space.
- The goal of exposure therapy is to reduce the fear and anxiety associated with the trigger.
- Your child might begin by creating a fear ladder. Then face their fear in their imagination with virtual reality or other forms of therapy and progress to real-life exposure.
- Your child will also learn coping mechanisms like breathing exercises and relaxation techniques.
- You need to understand the process and seek assistance from a professional to help your child succeed in exposure therapy.
- Some aspects to consider when choosing a therapist are:

  - Does the therapist have experience working with children?
  - What is the therapist's success rate?
  - What are the therapist's qualifications?
  - Do they accept health insurance?
  - Do they offer a copy of their plan/protocol?
  - Are you and your child comfortable with the therapist?

Along with exposure therapy, the therapist may assign homework or practices for you to incorporate at home, such as:

- Practice the exposure therapy techniques at home with your child.
- Use positive reinforcement to encourage your child, including verbal praise, stickers, or other rewards.
- Help your child identify their thoughts and feelings around their anxiety.
- Limit the time spent on screens.
- Encourage your child to get outside and be active.
- Make sure your child is sleeping enough every night.

You now have the tools you need to help your child overcome their anxiety. Your child can lead a happy and healthy life with the right support and treatment. Here are a few more success stories to help inspire you on your journey:

According to Effective Therapy Solutions, 16-year-old David was petrified of going to school because he was convinced his peers would make fun of him. His parents, worried about pressuring him, let him stay home at first. However, it became increasingly difficult to convince David even to leave the house. He had missed the first few weeks of school before his parents called a therapist.

David described himself as a shy boy and, over the last two years, that shyness became more like anxiety. He was nervous about saying something "dumb" or "stupid" in class and would constantly worry about what other people thought of him. When he would speak to his classmates, he would trip over his words, or he would blurt out something and then immediately regret it.

His heart would race, and his voice shook with nerves. It became difficult to hold a conversation. However, with the help of his therapist, the school counselor, his parents, and, of course, David's own courage, he could eventually return to school, and he even made some friends. He learned coping mechanisms and exposed himself to awkward situations until he felt more comfortable. He could finally take control of his anxiety.

As another example, an anonymous young woman shared that she had experienced obsessive thoughts since she was about nine or ten years old. At first, it began with smaller concerns, like believing she didn't know how to read or thought she was cheating on her homework by not reading. As a result, she would read out loud so she wouldn't miss anything. Then her worries became excessively worse.

At ten years old, she spent all night worrying about whether she had urinated in the pond at summer camp. Then she was concerned about being racist. She feared accidentally writing something racist and handing it to her seventh-grade African American teacher. After spending months trying to control her face, she gave a black girl a dirty look. She was devastated and punished herself by refusing to eat the candy letters on the family birthday cake.

Over time, these worries grew worse. When she was about eleven, she began babysitting and worried she would molest the child—a fear that carried into her adult years. Finally, she confessed to her parents, who only convinced her that her thoughts were a repercussion of overthinking and overanalyzing. Throughout her teen years and early adulthood, she tried different therapists, medications, and self-help groups with little to no success.

At one point, her fears grew exponentially, and even though she had a wonderful boyfriend, lots of friends, and a great job, she was concerned about robbing people or pushing people into traffic. These negative thoughts consumed her, and she locked herself in her home—safely away from anyone she might hurt.

However, it wasn't until she tried exposure therapy that things turned around. With the help of her therapist, she could face her fears head-on and eventually conquer them. First, she started with minor challenges like moving a leaf into someone's path or placing bottles near stairs, but she wasn't able to double-check if anyone was affected. As she grew more comfortable, she climbed up the ladder to her fear of molestation. She would walk around crowded areas, brush the shoulders of others, or stand a few feet away from people she thought she would harm.

Over time, she began writing note cards that tracked her "spikes" that helped her to better understand her triggers. With this knowledge, she could eventually gain control over her anxiety and accept that there are "risks" she would be taking. It took her a year and a half, but she's now able to live a relatively normal life. She continues to put her newfound practices to use and can even help others who have anxiety.

While these two examples are different, they both share a few key similarities. In both cases, the individuals felt like they had no control over their anxiety. They were consumed by their negative thoughts, affecting every area of their lives. However, with the help of a therapist and exposure therapy, they could eventually gain control of themselves and lead a fulfilling life.

If your child is experiencing anxiety, don't hesitate to get help. Early intervention is essential when helping your child develop the techniques they need to manage their anxiety and live more confidently. This book has everything you need for you and your child(ren) to start on the right foot. If you found this helpful, please leave a review and share it with a friend. Thank you for reading!

AUTHOR AND PUBLISHER'S NOTE

Thank you for reading one of my books. I have a total of two books so far, which is a great feat for I just started in the writing and publishing business in July of 2022.

For the past 11 years, I worked in the corporate world. On July 2022, I resigned from my stable position in the private education sector. What was I supposed to do next? I knew that I did not want to be in the corporate world anymore. I searched the internet for various side hustles that would nurture my artistic side while supporting my family.

Whoa! There is so much information that weeding through it was a tedious task. After a few weeks of research, I came across a publishing course and an e-Commerce course. Now I am an independent author and publisher, and business owner. My husband and I now have our own business called

LightTight LLC. It is still in its infancy, but we are so proud to take this humongous step forward in the second chapter of our lives. It was not an easy decision to step away from a stable job, but I am overjoyed by the risk and the rewards I have encountered doing these two new ventures. I majored in English with a concentration in Advertising/Marketing but never thought I would end up using my degree. I am thankful for my family and friends, and for readers like you for supporting me in my quest to publish books that will benefit many readers.

Thank you for joining me in telling the story about how exposure therapy can help your child take control of their anxiety disorders, phobias, and OCD within 10 weeks.

If you loved the book and have 60 seconds to spare, I would really appreciate a short review on Amazon. Your help in spreading the word about exposure therapy is greatly appreciated.

https://is.gd/3yxmos

I love hearing from my readers, and I personally read every single review.

Thank you!

Lulu James

P.S. If you'd like to know when my next book comes out and want to receive occasional updates, please email me at

lulujames@lighttightstory.com.

REFERENCES

Ackerman, E. (2021, March 4). *The benefits of art therapy for children*. Impaq Education. https://www.impaq.co.za/the-benefits-of-art-therapy-for-children/

Adilah. (n.d.). *Why Parents should never Force their Kids into Doing Anything*. MyPrivateTutor Malaysia Blog. https://www.myprivatetutor.my/blog/why-parents-should-never-force-their-kids-into-doing-anything

Albrecht, K. (2012). *The (Only) 5 Fears We All Share*. Psychology Today. https://www.psychologytoday.com/us/blog/brainsnacks/201203/the-only-5-fears-we-all-share

American Psychological Association. (2017a). Prolonged Exposure (PE). *Https://www.apa.org*. https://www.apa.org/ptsd-guideline/treatments/prolonged-exposure

American Psychological Association. (2017b, July). What Is Exposure Therapy? *Https://www.apa.org*. https://www.apa.org/ptsd-guideline/patients-and-families/exposure-therapy

Antonia. (2021, February 15). *How to Create a Calm Home: 20 Tips for More Peace and Less Stress*. BALANCE through SIMPLICITY. https://balancethroughsimplicity.com/how-to-create-a-calm-family-home/

Anxiety Disorders in Adolescents: Rates and Statistics. (n.d.). Mission Harbor Behavioral Health. https://sbtreatment.com/program/adolescent/anxiety/

Babauta, L. (2019). *Learn to Respond, Not React: zen habits*. Zenhabits.net. https://zenhabits.net/respond/

Baliotis, V. (2014, June 30). *When Your Child Begins Therapy: Guidelines for Parents*. Dr. Vula Baliotis. https://www.drvula.com/child-begins-therapy-expect-guidelines-say-child/

Beck, M. (n.d.). *Motivational Quote by Martha Beck*. Www.insightoftheday.com. https://www.insightoftheday.com/motivational-quote-by-martha-beck-08-09-2020

Beecroft, L. (2019, May 29). *Negative Thinking Patterns: How To Manage, Inter-*

pret And Reframe. Mywellbeing.com. https://mywellbeing.com/therapy-101/how-to-better-manage-negative-thought-patterns

Benefits of Reiki for Children - New England Naturopathic Health. (n.d.). New England Naturopathic Health. https://www.naturopathicme.com/benefits-reiki-children/

Biofeedback for Kids. (n.d.). Children's Health Orange County. https://www.choc.org/programs-services/integrative-health/biofeedback-therapy/

Bobnar, A. (2015, March 24). *8 Calming or Stimulating Sensory Activities for Kids with Sensory Impairment | WonderBaby.org*. WonderBaby.org - Helping Your Baby Reach Greater Wonders. https://www.wonderbaby.org/articles/calming-or-stimulating-sensory-activities

Brown, L. C. (2009, May 27). *12 Tips for Teaching Teens - NAfME*. NAfME. https://nafme.org/12-tips-for-teaching-teens/

Bunche-Smith, T. (2019, April 30). *3 Ways to Teach Children (Age 2 to 6)*. WikiHow. https://www.wikihow.com/Teach-Children-(Age-2-to-6)

Bunting, U. (2021, May 7). *A Mother's Guide to Ayurveda for Healthy Kids*. Yoga Journal. https://www.yogajournal.com/lifestyle/health/ayurveda/ayurveda-kids/

Canadian Mental Health Association. (2015). *What's the difference between anxiety and an anxiety disorder? | Here to Help*. Heretohelp.bc.ca. https://www.heretohelp.bc.ca/q-and-a/whats-the-difference-between-anxiety-and-an-anxiety-disorder

CDC. (2019, May 1). *Anxiety and depression in children: Get the facts*. Centers for Disease Control and Prevention. https://www.cdc.gov/childrensmentalhealth/features/anxiety-depression-children.html

CECMHC | Ideas for Teaching Children about Emotions. (2020). Ecmhc.org. https://www.ecmhc.org/ideas/emotions.html

Cherney, K. (2020, August 25). *12 Effects of Anxiety on the Body*. Healthline. https://www.healthline.com/health/anxiety/effects-on-body

Chia, S. (2021, February 3). *15 Ways to improve your focus and concentration skills | BetterUp*. www.betterup.com. https://www.betterup.com/blog/15-ways-to-improve-your-focus-and-concentration-skills

Cleveland Clinic. (2019). *Diaphragmatic Breathing Exercises & Techniques | Cleveland Clinic*. Cleveland Clinic. https://my.clevelandclinic.org/health/articles/9445-diaphragmatic-breathing

Cullinan, C. C. (2018). *Taking Your Child to a Therapist (for Parents) - KidsHealth.* Kidshealth.org. https://kidshealth.org/en/parents/finding-therapist.html

Cullins, A. (2017). *25 Things You Can Do Right Now To Build a Child's Confidence.* Big Life Journal. https://biglifejournal.com/blogs/blog/child-confidence

Dance/Movement Therapy | Children's Hospital Colorado. (n.d.). www.childrens-colorado.org. https://www.childrenscolorado.org/doctors-and-depart ments/departments/child-life/ponzio-creative-arts-therapy/dance-movement-therapy/

David's Success Story. (n.d.). www.effectivetherapysolutions.com. https://www. effectivetherapysolutions.com/success-stories/success-story-david

Davidson, K. (2020, February 5). *Mood food: 9 foods that can really boost your spirits.* Healthline. https://www.healthline.com/nutrition/mood-food

Delagran, L. (2012). *Impact of Fear and Anxiety | Taking Charge of Your Health & Wellbeing.* Taking Charge of Your Health & Wellbeing. https://www. takingcharge.csh.umn.edu/impact-fear-and-anxiety

8 Soothing Techniques to Help Relieve Anxiety. (2020, April 24). Www.uhhospital-s.org. https://www.uhhospitals.org/Healthy-at-UH/articles/2020/04/8-soothing-techniques-to-help-relieve-anxiety

Evans, A. (2021, May 19). *How to Make A Calm Down Box in 5 Minutes (for Kids and Adults) -.* ChildSavers. https://www.childsavers.org/calm-down-box/

Expect, W. to. (2018, November 2). *What to Expect in the First Therapy Session for Kids and Teens.* Montreal Therapy Centre. https://www.montrealther apy.com/expect-first-therapy-session-kids-teens/

Ferguson, M. (n.d.). *A quote by Marilyn Ferguson.* Www.goodreads.com. https:// www.goodreads.com/quotes/83783-ultimately-we-know-deeply-that-the-other-side-of-every

Fight Or Flight Response. (2021). Psychology Tools. https://www.psychology tools.com/resource/fight-or-flight-response/

Florida Behavioral Health. (2019, August 6). *4 Ways That Untreated Anxiety Impacts Physical Health | FLBH Blog.* Behavioral Health Florida. https://www.behav ioralhealthflorida.com/blog/4-ways-untreated-anxiety-physical-health/

Frequently Asked Questions. (n.d.). Www.effectivetherapysolutions.com. https:// www.effectivetherapysolutions.com/our-approach/frequently-asked-questions

Gavin, M. (2018). *Kids and Exercise (for Parents) - KidsHealth*. Kidshealth.org. https://kidshealth.org/en/parents/exercise.html

Gavin, M. L. (2016). *All About Sleep (for Parents)*. Kidshealth.org. https://kidshealth.org/en/parents/sleep.html

Generalized Anxiety Disorder GAD | Boston Children's Hospital. (n.d.). www.childrenshospital.org. https://www.childrenshospital.org/conditions/generalized-anxiety-disorder-gad

Glowiak, M. (2022, January 19). *Zoophobia (Fear of Animals): Symptoms, Treatments, & How to Cope*. Choosing Therapy. https://www.choosingtherapy.com/zoophobia/

Graduate Story #8. (n.d.). Ccbp. https://www.cognitivebehavioralcenter.com/gs8

Green, J. (n.d.). *Julien Green Quotes*. BrainyQuote. https://www.brainyquote.com/quotes/julien_green_192101

Haine-Schlagel, R., & Walsh, N. E. (2015). A Review of Parent Participation Engagement in Child and Family Mental Health Treatment. *Clinical Child and Family Psychology Review, 18*(2), 133–150. https://doi.org/10.1007/s10567-015-0182-x

Hall, K.-M. (2021, October 25). *Fear vs. Phobia: What Are They, and Is There a Difference?* GoodRx. https://www.goodrx.com/health-topic/mental-health/fear-vs-phobia

Hashimi, B. (2017, April 12). Scare tactic leaves damaging impact on children's future. *Pajhwok.com*. https://pajhwok.com/2017/04/12/scare-tactic-leaves-damaging-impact-childrens-future/

How Do I Find a Good Therapist? (2022). Apa.org. https://www.apa.org/ptsd-guideline/patients-and-families/finding-good-therapist.

How is OCD Treated? - OCD in Kids. (2019). OCD in Kids. https://kids.iocdf.org/what-is-ocd-kids/how-is-ocd-treated/

How to choose the right therapist. (2010, November 3). Health24. https://www.news24.com/health24/medical/depression/psychotherapy/how-to-choose-the-right-therapist-20120721

Hypnotherapy for Children | The Gut Centre. (n.d.). Www.thegutcentre.com. https://www.thegutcentre.com/treatment/hypnotherapy/hypnotherapy-for-children

Jacobson, R. (2021, August 16). *How to Help Children Manage Fears*. Child Mind Institute. https://childmind.org/article/help-children-manage-fears/

Janardhan Reddy, Y. C., Sundar, A. S., Narayanaswamy, J. C., & Math, S. B. (2017). Clinical practice guidelines for Obsessive-Compulsive Disorder. *Indian Journal of Psychiatry, 59*(Suppl 1), S74–S90. https://doi.org/10.4103/0019-5545.196976

John, P. (2022, June 29). *Virtual Reality Exposure Therapy: How It Works & Who It's Right For.* Choosing Therapy. https://www.choosingtherapy.com/virtual-reality-exposure-therapy/

Johnson, A. (2014, July 10). *Acupuncture for Kids.* Intermountainhealthcare.org. https://intermountainhealthcare.org/blogs/topics/research/2014/07/acupuncture-for-kids/

Keller, H. (n.d.). *A quote by Helen Keller.* Www.goodreads.com. https://www.goodreads.com/quotes/5100318-optimism-is-the-faith-that-leads-to-achievement-nothing-can

Kid Friendly Foods That Ease Anxiety. (n.d.). Www.brainbalancecenters.com. https://www.brainbalancecenters.com/blog/kid-friendly-foods-ease-anxiety

Kids doing TRE. (2021, May 11). Jodi-Anne's Insights into Peace and Happiness. https://www.jodiannemsmith.com/kids-doing-tre/

Kounang, N. (2015, October 29). *What is the science behind fear?* CNN. https://www.cnn.com/2015/10/29/health/science-of-fear/

Lesnak, E. (2017, February 3). *4 reasons your child should see a naturopathic doctor.* Dr. Emily Lesnak. http://www.dremilylesnak.com/new-blog/2016/8/21/5-reasons-to-have-a-naturopathic-doctor-on-your-childs-care-team

Logan-Banks, P. (2022). *How to teach your child to be responsible.* BabyCentre UK. https://www.babycentre.co.uk/a1021954/how-to-teach-your-child-to-be-responsible

Lyness, D. (2018a, July). *Your Child's Self-Esteem (for Parents) - KidsHealth.* Kidshealth.org. https://kidshealth.org/en/parents/self-esteem.html

Lyness, D. (2018b, October). *Normal Childhood Fears.* Kidshealth.org. https://kidshealth.org/en/parents/anxiety.html

McArdle, J. (2014, August 24). *Perception of fear vs reality of danger.* Stuff. https://www.stuff.co.nz/stuff-nation/assignments/have-you-overcome-your-greatest-fear/10412343/Perception-of-fear-vs-reality-of-danger

McGee, J. B. (2013). *A quote from Skipping Stones.* Www.goodreads.com.

https://www.goodreads.com/quotes/894045-i-ve-learned-through-the-years-that-it-s-not-where-you

McLernon, L. M. (2021, August 9). *Depression and anxiety doubled in children, pandemic study says.* CIDRAP. https://www.cidrap.umn.edu/news-perspective/2021/08/depression-and-anxiety-doubled-children-pandemic-study-says

McNeill, B. (2019, May 9). *Facing fears: How exposure therapy can help children with anxiety.* VCU News. https://news.vcu.edu/article/Facing_fears_How_exposure_therapy_can_help_children_with_anxiety

Monroe, M. (n.d.). *A quote from Marilyn.* Www.goodreads.com. https://www.goodreads.com/quotes/645741-just-because-you-fail-once-it-doesn-t-mean-you-re-going

Morgan, J. (2021, December 15). *4 Tips To Embrace Your Mistakes.* Jacob Morgan. https://thefutureorganization.com/4-tips-to-embrace-your-mistakes/

Morin, A. (2020, December 14). *Prevent Behavior Problems by Teaching Your Child About Feelings.* Verywell Family. https://www.verywellfamily.com/how-to-teach-kids-about-feelings-1095012

Morin, A. (2021, August 29). *How Sand Tray Therapy Heals Psychological Wounds.* Verywell Mind. https://www.verywellmind.com/what-is-sand-tray-therapy-4589493

MUSIC THERAPY AND YOUNG CHILDREN. (n.d.). https://www.musictherapy.org/assets/1/7/MT_Young_Children_2006.pdf

Music Therapy Success Stories with Special Needs Children. (2016, February 27). Harmony Music Therapy. https://harmonymusictherapy.com/music-therapy-success-stories-with-special-needs-children/

Northwestern Medicine. (2021). *The Truth Behind Fear.* Northwestern Medicine. https://www.nm.org/healthbeat/healthy-tips/emotional-health/5-things-you-never-knew-about-fear

Nyctophobia (Fear of the Dark): Symptoms & Causes. (2022, March 28). Cleveland Clinic. https://my.clevelandclinic.org/health/diseases/22785-nyctophobia-fear-of-the-dark

Obsessive-Compulsive Disorder In Children And Adolescents. (2018, October). www.aacap.org. https://www.aacap.org/AACAP/Families_and_Youth/Facts_for_Families/FFF-Guide/Obsessive-Compulsive-Disorder-In-Children-And-Adolescents-060.aspx

OCD Cognitive Behavior Therapy Success Stories. (n.d.). Advanced Behavioral Health. https://behaviortherapynyc.com/success-stories-ocd/

Owens, J. (2015, May 18). *Anxious Child? Here are 5 Supplements for Anxiety.* AT: Parenting Survival for All Ages. https://www.anxioustoddlers.com/supplements-childhood-anxiety/#.YxXNtXbMK5c

Paradigmtreat. (2021, December 23). *Teen Fears and Phobias: A Guide for Parents.* Paradigm Treatment. https://paradigmtreatment.com/teen-fears-and-phobias-guide-parents/

Parents Editor. (2015, June 11). *9 Secrets of Confident Kids.* Parents. https://www.parents.com/toddlers-preschoolers/development/fear/secrets-of-confident-kids/

Philpott, S. (2013, March 20). *Pregnancy, Parenting, Lifestyle, Beauty: Tips & Advice | mom.com.* Mom.com. https://mom.com/kids/6486-teaching-kids-about-thoughts-feelings-and-behaviors

Phobias in Children | Cedars-Sinai. (2019). Cedars-Sinai.org. https://www.cedars-sinai.org/health-library/diseases-and-conditions---pediatrics/p/phobias-in-children.html

Pietrangelo, A. (2019a, October 11). *Play Therapy: What Is It, How It Works, and Techniques.* Healthline. https://www.healthline.com/health/play-therapy

Pietrangelo, A. (2019b, December 5). *Cognitive Behavioral Therapy (CBT) for Kids: How It Works.* Healthline. https://www.healthline.com/health/mental-health/cbt-for-kids

Przeworski, A. (2014, May 30). *Facing Fears Without Pushing Your Child Over the Edge | Psychology Today.* www.psychologytoday.com. https://www.psychologytoday.com/us/blog/dont-worry-mom/201405/facing-fears-without-pushing-your-child-over-the-edge

Reichard, E. (2019, June 8). *Learn to Respond, Not React | Safety Blog | Tradebe USA.* www.tradebe.com. https://www.tradebe.com/blog/safety/learn-to-respond-not-react

Rodgers, M. (2004, June). *Hannah, an anxious child | ADAVIC Anxiety Disorders Association of Victoria, Inc.* www.adavic.org.au. https://www.adavic.org.au/PG-articles-hannah-an-anxious-child.aspx

Rothbaum, B. (2020a, September 14). *8 Myths About Exposure Therapy.* Psychotherapy Academy. https://psychotherapyacademy.org/pe-trauma-training-ptsd/8-myths-about-exposure-therapy/

Rothbaum, B. (2020b, September 17). *PE Therapy Sessions: Structure and Main*

Components. Psychotherapy Academy. https://psychotherapyacademy.org/pe-trauma-training-ptsd/pe-therapy-sessions-structure-and-main-components/

Sandy's Success Story. (n.d.). www.effectivetherapysolutions.com. https://www.effectivetherapysolutions.com/success-stories/success-story-sandy

Schwartz, S. (2016, March 15). *5 Foods To Calm Your Kids*. Ecohappiness Project. https://ecohappinessproject.com/5-foods-to-calm-your-kids/

Scott, E. (2019). *The Benefits of Box Breathing for Stress Management*. Verywell Mind. https://www.verywellmind.com/the-benefits-and-steps-of-box-breathing-4159900

Scott, S. J. (2019, January 12). *How to Be More Self Aware: 8 Tips to Boost Self-Awareness*. Develop Good Habits. https://www.developgoodhabits.com/what-is-self-awareness/

Smith, A. (2017). *Zen Out With Your Kids: How to Introduce Meditation to Children | Mindfulness*. 30Seconds Health. https://30seconds.com/health/tip/14102/Zen-Out-With-Your-Kids-How-to-Introduce-Meditation-to-Children

Smith, E. (2021, August 3). *How You Can Create A Calm Environment At Home*. The Best of This Life. https://www.bestofthislife.com/2021/08/create-calm-environment-at-home.html

Smith, L. (2017, November 10). *How to Be a Master of your own thoughts by Following these Simple Rules*. YourStory.com. https://yourstory.com/mystory/740900dd3e-how-to-be-a-master-of/amp

Smith, S. G. (2018, January 4). *4 Reasons Why Exposure Therapy May Not Be Working*. Stacysmithcounseling. https://www.stacysmithcounseling.com/post/reasons-why-exposure-therapy-may-not-be-working

Sorensen, D. (2022, April 20). *How to ask for help | Psyche Guides*. Psyche. https://psyche.co/guides/how-to-ask-for-help-without-discomfort-or-apology

Spurgeon, C. H. (n.d.). *A quote by Charles Haddon Spurgeon*. Www.goodreads.com. https://www.goodreads.com/quotes/98356-our-anxiety-does-not-empty-tomorrow-of-its-sorrows-but

Staff, M. (2019, April 13). *How to meditate*. Mindful. https://www.mindful.org/how-to-meditate/

Stanborough, R. J. (2020, August 17). *9 Tips for Finding the Right Therapist*. Healthline. https://www.healthline.com/health/how-to-find-a-therapist

Stop Praising Kids And Do This Instead. (2018, May 3). Kiddie Matters. https://www.kiddiematters.com/stop-praising-kids-and-do-this-instead/

The Importance of Celebrating Your Child's Successes. (2018, May 15). Applied Behavioral Consulting | ABA & Other Autism Therapies. https://www.abctherapyclinics.com/the-importance-of-celebrating-your-childs-successes/

Tilak, V. (2014, August 5). *The Benefits of Yoga for Kids.* Parents. https://www.parents.com/fun/sports/exercise/the-benefits-of-yoga-for-kids/

Timms, M. (2022, February 9). *Blame Culture Is Toxic. Here's How to Stop It.* Harvard Business Review. https://hbr.org/2022/02/blame-culture-is-toxic-heres-how-to-stop-it

12 Tips to Raise Confident Children | Building Self-Esteem. (2022, April 15). Child Mind Institute. https://childmind.org/article/12-tips-raising-confident-kids/

20 Ways to Celebrate Accomplishments with Your Family. (2016, March 8). Together Counts. https://togethercounts.com/20-ways-to-celebrate-accomplishments-with-your-family/

Valentine, K. (2021, May 6). *Here's the Key Difference Between OCD and Anxiety.* NOCD. https://www.treatmyocd.com/blog/is-ocd-a-form-of-anxiety

Vinall, M. (2021, March 11). *Mantras for Anxiety: Harness the Healing Power of Chanting to Ease Fear, Stress, and Depression.* Healthline. https://www.healthline.com/health/mind-body/mantras-for-anxiety

WebMD Editorial Contributors. (2020, November 23). *Signs of Fear.* WebMD. https://www.webmd.com/mental-health/signs-of-fear

When Do Minors in Therapy Have a Right to Confidentiality? (2019, September 27). www.goodtherapy.org. https://www.goodtherapy.org/for-professionals/software-technology/hipaa-security/article/when-do-minors-in-therapy-have-a-right-to-confidentiality

Willard, C. (2020, June 11). *Mindfulness for Kids.* Mindful. https://www.mindful.org/mindfulness-for-kids/

Winfrey, O. (n.d.). *A quote by Oprah Winfrey.* Www.goodreads.com. https://www.goodreads.com/quotes/2646-the-more-you-praise-and-celebrate-your-life-the-more

Wright, J. (2021, August 25). *How to Talk to Children.* WikiHow. https://www.wikihow.com/Talk-to-Children

Yetman, D. (2021, June 21). *Exposure Therapy: Types, How It's Done, and More.*

Healthline. https://www.healthline.com/health/exposure-therapy#conditions

You Are What You Think: How Your Thoughts Create Your Reality. (2020, April 21). OMAR ITANI. https://www.omaritani.com/blog/what-you-think

Zafar |, S. (2022, May 12). *Types of Natural Disaster-Related Phobias and How To Get Help.* BioEnergy Consult. https://www.bioenergyconsult.com/natural-disaster-related-phobias-and-how-to-get-help/

Zenhabits. (2007, July 25). *12 Ideas for Establishing a Calming Routine.* Zen Habits. https://zenhabits.net/12-ideas-for-establishing-a-calming-routine/

IMAGE REFERENCES

Asangbam, D. (2020, December 11). *Photo by Dev Asangbam on Unsplash.* Unsplash.com. https://unsplash.com/photos/_sh9vkVbVgo

Collins, R. (2017, August 7). *Photo by Robert Collins on Unsplash.* Unsplash.com. https://unsplash.com/photos/tvc5imO5pXk

Ebrahim, A. (2019, April 8). *Photo by Andrew Ebrahim on Unsplash.* Unsplash.com. https://unsplash.com/photos/zRwXf6PizEo

Fratila, S. (2018, November 8). *Photo by sabina fratila on Unsplash.* Unsplash.com. https://unsplash.com/photos/SZqZu4NQsak

Fuhrman, L. (2018, June 9). *Photo by Laura Fuhrman on Unsplash.* Unsplash.com. https://unsplash.com/photos/dEVHukGkHq4

Gontariu, D. (2019, June 13). *Photo by Dragos Gontariu on Unsplash.* Unsplash.com. https://unsplash.com/photos/54VAb3f1z6w

Heftiba, T. (2021, February 4). *Photo by Toa Heftiba on Unsplash.* Unsplash.com. https://unsplash.com/photos/XIAJd448FnY

JodyHongFilms. (2017, June 1). *Photo by JodyHongFilms on Unsplash.* Unsplash.com. https://unsplash.com/photos/sl1mbxJFFpU

Kazuend. (2016, September 5). *Photo by kazuend on Unsplash.* Unsplash.com. https://unsplash.com/photos/FnyVCcmTodQ

Libralon, S. (2018, February 22). *Photo by Steven Libralon on Unsplash.* Unsplash.com. https://unsplash.com/photos/Do1GQljlNk8

Lissa, W. (2017, September 2). *Photo by Wadi Lissa on Unsplash.* Unsplash.com. https://unsplash.com/photos/4U1x6459Q-s

Lucas, J. (2021, September 17). *Photo by Jack Lucas Smith on Unsplash.* Unsplash.com. https://unsplash.com/photos/Zxq0dvmRyIo

Naddam, Y. (2018, November 11). *Help yourself ! | HD photo by youssef naddam (@youssefnaddam) on Unsplash.* Unsplash.com; Unsplash. https://unsplash.com/photos/iJ2IG8ckCpA

Perera, R. (2021, January 24). *Photo by Rajiv Perera on Unsplash.* Unsplash.com. https://unsplash.com/photos/_JjYYsQPneE

Rice, J. (2017, September 22). *Photo by Jared Rice on Unsplash.* Unsplash.com. https://unsplash.com/photos/NTyBbu66_SI

Rosewell, J. (2016, January 25). *Photo by Jason Rosewell on Unsplash.* Unsplash.com. https://unsplash.com/photos/ASKeuOZqhYU

Tyson. (2021, July 30). *Photo by Tyson on Unsplash.* Unsplash.com. https://unsplash.com/photos/UxTrmMqD2Dk

Wedemeyer, B. (2020, July 26). *Photo by Benjamin Wedemeyer on Unsplash.* Unsplash.com. https://unsplash.com/photos/FQGG3ES_3jI

Whitt, J. (2016, October 4). *Photo by Jordan Whitt on Unsplash.* Unsplash.com. https://unsplash.com/photos/KQCXf_zvdaU

Zhao, J. (2021, January 28). *Photo by Jacky Zhao on Unsplash.* Unsplash.com. https://unsplash.com/photos/nfVMgrQlBHI